The Vegetarian GOURMET

Judy Ridgway

Prentice-Hall, Inc., Englewood Cliffs, N.J. 07632 A SPECTRUM BOOK

Library of Congress Cataloging in Publication Data

RIDGWAY, JUDY.
    The vegetarian gourmet.

    (A Spectrum Book)
    Includes bibliographical references and index.
    1.–Vegetarian cookery.   2.–Nutrition.   I.–Title.
TX837.R53   641.5'636   80-24420
ISBN 0-13-941492-4
ISBN 0-13-941484-3 (pbk.)

© 1981 by Judy Ridgway

Illustrations © 1981 by Ward Lock Ltd, London

Editorial/production supervision and interior design
by Donald Chanfrau

Cover and insert color photography
by Edmund Goldspink and Orbis Verlag

Manufacturing buyer: Barbara A. Frick

Front jacket: Ratatouille Roulade and Glazed Vegetable Pate
Back jacket: Artichoke Dip, Mexican Dip, and Indian Curry Dip

A SPECTRUM BOOK

10   9   8   7   6   5   4   3   2   1

Printed in the United States of America

PRENTICE-HALL INTERNATIONAL, INC., *London*
PRENTICE-HALL OF AUSTRALIA PTY. LIMITED, *Sydney*
PRENTICE-HALL OF CANADA, LTD., *Toronto*
PRENTICE-HALL OF INDIA PRIVATE LIMITED, *New Delhi*
PRENTICE-HALL OF JAPAN, INC., *Tokyo*
PRENTICE-HALL OF SOUTHEAST ASIA PTE. LTD., *Singapore*
WHITEHALL BOOKS LIMITED, *Wellington, New Zealand*

Contents

Eating Vegetarian 1

There is no doubt about it—you are what you eat. After all, food both liquid and solid is the only source of all the materials that the body needs to keep it in good working order, to grow, and to rebuild itself. The food you eat not only affects your health but also your personality and your behavior. If your health is poor and your body is trying desperately to cope with the effects of a bad diet, you are unlikely to feel on top of the world and your ability to deal with the ups and downs of everyday life will be impaired. You will probably feel tired and sluggish with a tendency to snap at the slightest provocation.

On the other hand if your body is working well and you feel in peak condition, your mental state will usually benefit as well. You will feel much more alert and able to cope.

The connection between health and nutrition is an extremely complicated one. In cases of extreme deficiency there are obvious symptoms of disease such as scurvy in the case of vitamin C deficiency and beriberi in the case of vitamin B deficiency. But in most Western countries the diet is a varied one, and on the whole people seem to be reasonably well fed.

Nevertheless, a number of "new" diseases have appeared or have greatly increased over the last two or three generations and some of them, at least, seem to be related to diet. They include coronary heart disease, obesity, and diseases of the bowel.

1

All these considerations make it extremely important to understand the basics of nutrition—particularly when eating vegetarian means cutting out a substantial source of available food in the form of meat and fish.

Basic nutritional requirements

There are a number of essential materials that the body needs to function properly and these are known as nutrients. Many of them are found in different sorts of food and in theory it doesn't matter which kind of food you get them from provided that you get them. Others are only available in a limited number of foods, and some of these can cause slight problems for vegetarians and even greater problems for vegeans who also exclude all dairy produce from their diet.

One of these is iron, which, although it is present in eggs, bread and vegetables, is often not in the form that the body can easily absorb. However, this can be overcome by drinking fruit juice, which is rich in vitamin C, at the same time as eating the iron containing food. The presence of vitamin C helps the body to change the iron into a form that can be assimilated more easily.

Another problem nutrient, particularly for vegeans, is vitamin B12. This is thought to occur only in foods of animal origin, particularly liver, kidneys, sardines, and herring. However, the vegetarian can get it from eggs, milk, and cheese. But the vegean will have to resort to supplementary tablets of synthesized vitamin.

The essential nutrients are made up of proteins, carbohydrates, and fats plus a variety of vitamins and mineral salts.

Proteins

Protein is, apart from water, the largest single constituent of the body. Indeed 17% of the body tissues are made up of protein. So the protein you eat is a major source of material for growth and tissue replacement. At first glance this might seem to be much more important for children than for adults, and this is indeed partially the case. But the body is continuously renewing itself and replacing tissues and so adults, too, need a regular supply of protein in the diet. Any excess protein supplied to the body is used as a source of energy and burnt off in activity or stored in the form of glycogen and fat.

Major sources of protein are meat, fish, eggs, cheese, pulses (which are types of beans, peas, lentils), nuts, and seeds. The first two, of course, are not available to the vegetarian, but the alternative sources provide a wide choice of protein-rich food. Minor sources of proteins are bread, cereals, rice, and pasta. In fact, almost all food, with the exception of pure fat and pure sugar, contains some protein—even inner parts of vegetables and cabbage leaves contain protein, although these are poor sources of protein percentage-wise. However, if you eat enough of them they could contribute significant quantities of protein to the diet.

Of course, the various protein sources differ in the type of proteins they provide, and these differences affect the amount of usable protein available to the body. These and other factors, such as the amount of protein required by the body and theory of complementary proteins, are discussed in Chapter 2.

Carbohydrates

Pure carbohydrate is the only nutrient that provides energy alone and contributes nothing else. For this reason, carbohydrates are always blamed as the most "fattening" of foods. If the body takes in more energy as food than it can use up, then the surplus is converted into reserve stores in the unwelcome form of adipose tissue, or "fat."

However, with the exception of sugar, most carbohydrate foods are extremely useful sources of other nutrients. Two slices of bread, for example, provide a significant proportion of the body's daily protein requirement as well as supplies of calcium, iron, and vitamin B. Whole wheat bread is also an important source of vitamin E and a variety of minerals. Whole wheat pasta and brown rice are also useful sources of protein and other nutrients, and scrubbed, unpeeled new potatoes can contain as much as two-thirds of an adult's daily vitamin C requirement.

Fats

Fats are potentially much more fattening than carbohydrates as weight for weight they can produce about twice the amount of energy. They contain a number of vitamins including A, D, E, and K. They are present in a variety of foods such as milk, meat, cakes, and herring, as well as being obvious in foods such as butter, margarine, and cooking oil.

When fats are eaten they are broken down during digestion into glycerine and fatty acids. These fatty acids are divided into two groups depending on the number of hydrogen atoms in their makeup. Fatty acids having their full quota of hydrogen atoms are called saturated fatty acids, and those with four or more hydrogen atoms missing are called polyunsaturated fatty acids.

The latter group contains three fatty acids that the body is unable to manufacture for itself. These are required for growth and for the healthy development of cells and are therefore known as essential fatty acids. At one time they were incorrectly known as vitamin F. To date no generally accepted cases have been discovered of anyone suffering from a deficiency of essential fatty acids, although some nutritionists believe that such deficiencies are actually more common than is generally appreciated.

The main source of polyunsaturated fatty acids are certain specific vegetable oils such as safflower, corn, and soya bean. Minor sources include lean meat and poultry. Saturated fats are found in dairy produce, visible fat on meat, hard margarine, and other vegetable oils.

The exact role that each type of fat plays in the body is not fully understood, although it has been suggested that the ratio of the two types of fat consumed in the diet might have a part to play in the incidence of coronary heart disease, and this is discussed in more detail later in this chapter.

Most authorities agree, however, that people in the highly industrialized Western societies eat far more fat than their bodies need, either for body building or for energy. The average person probably eats about 100–120 grams (about 4 oz) of fat a day, which provides 40–50% of the energy in the diet. Advice offered by medical experts suggests that this percentage should be cut to around 35–40%. More than this would be difficult. Quite apart from the body's needs, fats play an important role in the diet as they carry much of the flavor of foods. They also improve the texture and assist in swallowing by lubricating the food.

Vitamins
Vitamins are present in our food in extremely small quantities, yet their absence can cause major deficiency symptoms. The biochemical function of most vitamins in the B group has been discovered, but full details are not known about the functions of vitamins A, D, and E, and there are many gaps in the knowledge about other vitamins.

A brief outline of the current knowledge of the functions of the principle vitamins is given below, together with their vegetarian sources.

Vitamin A
> Aids growth and protects moist tissues like the eyes, throat, and lungs.
> Found in butter, margarine, carrots, spinach, watercress, and apricots.

Vitamin B Complex
> Assists in converting food into usable materials for body building or energy.
> Found in bread, milk, dairy products, yeast, and green leafy vegetables.

Vitamins B1, B2, and niacin are soluble in water and can be lost in cooking simply by being washed out into the water.

Vitamin C

Aids healing and resistance to infection and keeps connective tissues in good repair. Aids in the assimilation of iron.

Found in oranges, lemons, black currants, peppers, cauliflower, potatoes, peas, cabbage, spinach, and watercress.

Is destroyed to some extent by heat.

Vitamin D

Aids healthy bone development.

Found in margarine, eggs, and butter.

Can be manufactured in the skin under the influence of sunlight.

Other essential vitamins include vitamins E and K. The precise role of these vitamins is not really understood, but vitamin E appears to be necessary for a healthy blood circulatory system and vitamin K is essential for blood clotting. Vitamin E is found in wheat germ and egg yolks and vitamin K in green vegetables and soya beans.

Mineral salts

Mineral salts form part of the body structure, and they also play a part in the functioning of the enzyme systems that affect all body processes.

Calcium and phosphate form the skeleton and are essential for healthy teeth, bones, and muscles. Iron is a constituent of the blood. Other mineral salts required are manganese, magnesium, copper, zinc, potassium, chloride, and sulphate. Most of these are needed in such small quantities that dietary deficiencies are thought to be rare.

Iron is found in bread, flour, cereal products, and apricots, as well as in some vegetables, and as mentioned above, mainly occurs in these sources in a form more easily assimilated in the presence of vitamin C.

Calcium is present in dairy products and bread, potassium in unpeeled potatoes and lima beans, and magnesium is found in cocoa, nuts, soya beans, whole grains, and leafy vegetables.

Many people believe that they must eat good red meat to supply all the vitamins and minerals that the body needs. But, in fact, nonmeat sources already provide more than half the normal intake of the eleven most frequently cited vitamins and minerals. By stepping up the intake of dairy and vegetable produce to replace meat in the diet, the vegetarian is also stepping up his or her intake of essential vitamins and minerals from these sources and is unlikely to experience any deficiency.

So what does all this mean in terms of everyday eating? There is no such thing as a perfect diet—rather there are many combinations of different foods that will provide all the nutrients that are required. Chapter 3 contains some guidelines on planning a balanced diet.

Because of the seeming adequacy of our Western diet, many nutritionists are avoiding the issue by simply advising people to "eat a little of everything and not too much of anything." This is fine as far as it goes, but scientists are beginning to understand some of the finer points of healthy eating, and it could be that more emphasis will need to be placed on the importance of eating certain types of food rather than others.

Why whole foods?

We are hearing more and more about whole foods these days. Magazine articles frequently suggest recipes using whole meal flour or brown rice, and an increasing number of supermarkets are stocking these products. Health food shops are opening up by the hundreds, and even the most conventional nutritionist reluctantly agrees that refining cereals to the extent that is now common practice means that they lose quite a high proportion of their nutrients.

Bread must be the classic example of a food that is refined to a detrimental degree. The standard white bread loaf contains about 70% extraction flour. A United Nations comparison of 100% whole wheat flour and 70% extraction flour shows that with the exception of carbohydrate, which is higher in white bread, all other nutrients are reduced.

	Whole Wheat	70% Extraction Flour
Protein percent in grams	12.2	11.3
Fat	2.4	1.6
Carbohydrate	64.1	72.0
Fiber	2.0	0.1
Thiamin mg (milligrams) per 100 g (grams)	0.37	0.08
Riboflavin	0.12	0.05
Nicotinic Acid	5.70	0.08
Iron	3.50	1.25

This table is by no means exhaustive and the same sort of dramatic reduction occurs with the other vitamins and minerals contained in whole wheat flour.

Admittedly calcium, vitamin B, nicotinic acid, and iron are added to the standard white loaf in an attempt to improve its nutritional value. But this ignores the other missing nutrients as well as the fact that the arrangement of what we eat before we eat it could affect what the body can do with it. Added nutrients may not have the same effect as those naturally contained in food.

Indeed there is serious cause to question all of the additives to our standard loaf and little reason to suppose that they are beneficial. For example, nicotinic acid is still added to bread despite the fact that it is now thought that the nicotinic acid used by the body does not come from cereals at all, but from totally different protein sources.

Nor is the iron added to bread in the easiest form for the body to assimilate, which might explain why, after twenty years of adding it to bread, there is no evidence to show it has had any effect whatsoever on the levels of anemia present in the population!

When wheat is milled and refined to white flour, it is the wheat germ and the husk that are lost. The wheat germ contains most of the cereal's nutrients, but nutritionists are coming around to the view that the loss of the husk is also detrimental, as the husk is extremely rich in dietary fiber.

Dietary fiber is really all those parts of the food that are not digested by the enzymes in the stomach and intestine and that pass through the system unchanged. It is considered by most experts to be important in the prevention of constipation and indeed of all kinds of digestive complaints from gallstones to diverticulitis. Some researchers are also beginning to think that it might have an important part to play in the prevention of heart disease and cancer.

The name *fiber* is a bit misleading as foods high in fiber are not necessarily stringy or fibrous. Even "smooth" foods like bananas contain some fiber. Whole wheat cereals of all kinds are particularly high in fiber content and so are fruit and vegetables, particularly peas, sweet corn, broccoli, and parsnips. Fiber is not affected by cooking so it is not necessary to eat raw food all the time to get sufficient dietary fiber.

If refining flour reduces the nutritional value of bread, the same argument holds good for anything made with that flour, whether it is made at home or in the factory. So it is probably worth thinking about buying whole wheat pasta and using whole wheat flour for baking and cooking. Rice is another cereal that loses a high proportion of its vitamin and fiber content when the husk is removed.

The other greatly refined food common in our diet

is, of course, white sugar. We need sugar, but this requirement could easily be met by eating other sugar-rich foods such as fruit. White sugar really doesn't contribute anything to the diet except excess energy and thus excess body fat.

Real brown sugar contains small amounts of potassium and calcium as well as traces of other minerals and vitamins. Molasses, being even less refined, contains the same things in even greater proportions. However, both brown sugar and molasses are still energy producers and they are also thought to be even worse for tooth decay than white sugar.

Honey contains only small quantities of minerals and few vitamins, but its constitution is different to the other sweeteners in that it is made up of glucose and fructose—the sugars found in fruit—rather than sucrose.

The various types of sugar seem to play different roles in the body chemistry and these are not really fully understood. They are, however, known to affect blood cholesterol levels, and some experts believe that sucrose could be a factor in the incidence of coronary heart disease.

Any discussion on whole foods must touch on the question of additives. Several thousands of chemical substances are currently added to foods during manufacture to preserve and flavor them to "improve" their color and texture. So far there has been no evidence to show that anyone has suffered any harm from permitted additives. But on the other hand there is no proof to the contrary, and the effect could be cumulative. Many processed foods have their contents printed on the label, and the choice is yours.

Some people carry their definition of whole foods beyond the questions of refining and additives to include only food that has been grown "organically" without the use of artificial fertilizers and hormones. Whether this is a valid distinction or merely a recipe for lining the pockets of the specialist growers and distributors is an argument beyond the scope of this book. However, fresh vegetables from the kitchen garden do have a flavor that seems to be absent from those found in most stores.

A question of cholesterol

In recent years there has been considerable emphasis on the connection between the amount of fat and cholesterol eaten in the diet, the concentration of cholesterol in the blood, and the incidence of coronary heart disease, with fats and cholesterol cast as the villains of the piece. Eating large quantities of foods rich in these items, said the experts, leads to high levels of blood cholesterol and from there to heart disease.

This theory was officially endorsed by United States and British groups. In fact, a 1976 report instigated by the Royal College of Physicians and the British Cardiac Society put the dietary blame for coronary heart disease firmly on saturated fats.

The reporting group examined evidence from a variety of sources, including population studies and field trials with dietary changes. The report stated that conclusive evidence for any particular dietary regime to reduce the incidence of heart disease was unlikely to emerge in the foreseeable future.

Yet despite this statement the report went on to recommend that everyone should not only reduce the overall amount of fat eaten, but they should replace some of their saturated fat intake with polyunsaturated fats, which, it was alleged, would help to counteract any buildup of cholesterol from other sources. The report gave specific details on how to achieve the changeover by cutting down on dairy produce and meat, and substituting poultry, fish, soft margarines, and oils rich in polyunsaturated fats. The recommended diet was even more stringent for those considered to be high risks.

The implication for vegetarians of such recommendations are enormous. Dairy produce is a major source of protein, not to mention a variety of vitamins and other nutrients and to cut them out at one fell swoop could lead to serious health problems. Such a diet, of course, is already followed by vegans, but considerable knowledge of the food values of vegetable produce is required if they are to remain really healthy.

However, not all authorities agree with such reports as this one, and some seriously question the evidence on which they are based. There is a growing body of opinion, backed by authoritative research, which alleges that fats in the diet do not have any causative role in the incidence of heart disease and that eggs and dairy produce are not harmful in normal quantities.

There are a number of reasons why cholesterol was thought to be a causative factor in heart disease. First, it has been known for a long time that arteries showing signs of hardening contain large amounts of fats in the build up of materials in the hardening walls and subsequent research showed that these fats included a high level of cholesterol. Second, patients who suffer from heart disease frequently have higher than average levels of blood cholesterol. Third, high blood cholesterol levels and hardening of the arteries may be induced in experimental animals by feeding them with lots of fat. Fourth, there is known to be a definite connection between the amount of animal fat consumed and the level of cholesterol in the blood. Taking all these factors together, it is easily concluded that a reduction in animal fat intake should reduce the probability of suffering from hardening of the arteries.

However, more recent research has shown that cholesterol is not present at the part of the hardening process, and many distinguished research workers who previously believed cholesterol to be a causative factor are changing their views. Some researchers go even further and state that the cholesterol present at the later stages might be the result of a repair function of cholesterol.

In addition, meticulously controlled trials of cholesterol-reducing diets carried out in the United States through the 1970s have failed to produce any difference in the recurrence of heart disease or in the ultimate death rate of patients. In each of the trials, the blood cholesterol was lowered quite significantly, and if it had been causative factor, a beneficial result would have been expected.

Advocates of the polyunsaturated fat diet state that there are no known disadvantages to the diet and that it might possibly be of help. However, it seems rather drastic to change the dietary habits of centuries on the basis of such poor evidence. There is also growing evidence to support the suggestion that lowering the blood cholesterol levels could increase the incidence and frequency of gallstones. After all cholesterol does have a number of essential functions in the body. These concern the absorption of fats into the blood stream and their transport to different parts of the body.

To carry out the transportation function, cholesterol combines with fats in the blood to form two substances, known as high-density lipids and low-density lipids. Research suggests that it is the ratio of these two substances in the blood that is the more useful index of the risk of developing coronary heart disease. And this ratio is not related to the type of fat in the diet. However, it *is* affected by smoking, exercise levels, and obesity—all known to be important factors in heart disease—and by the amount of carbohydrates in the diet.

Even more recent research has found evidence that a high intake of dietary fiber from cereals reduces the likelihood of suffering from coronary heart disease, although the mechanism behind this remains unexplained.

So it now looks as if there is no need to follow a strict diet of no saturated fats. However, people in general do eat far more fat than they need. So if you have even the slightest weight problem, it makes sense

to cut down on fats of all kinds, as well as on carbohydrates, and to step up the amount of exercise you
take so that you more nearly balance your energy
intake and output on a daily basis.

The energy balance

To some people the beans and cereals of a vegetarian
diet sound like a recipe for overweight. To others the
emphasis on vegetables seems like the road to starvation. Of course, neither of these extreme pictures is
correct. All the food we eat provides essential nutrients
and energy, and vegetarians are merely substituting
one set of food patterns for another. There is no
intrinsic reason why they should get fatter or thinner
than others provided that they get their energy balance
right. In fact, surveys have shown that despite the
seemingly high carbohydrate content of the diet, vegetarians are less likely to be fat than are meat eaters.

Fatness or obesity is a real problem in the Western
world, and it is not just the looks of the obese person
that are at stake. Obesity increases the risk of diabetes,
heart disease, gout, high blood pressure, bronchitis,
gallstones, and varicose veins. Fat people have a higher
accident rate and they die younger.

According to figures collected by the American
Society of Actuaries, a man over 45 years old, who is
11 kg (25 lb) overweight reduces his life expectancy by
25%. If he loses his excess weight, his life expectation
returns to normal—all very cogent reasons for trying
to keep one's weight down.

There is usually no intrinsic reason why a person
should be overweight provided that the energy balance
is maintained. The energy balance is quite simply the
difference between energy input in the form of food
and energy output in the form of activity. If these are
balanced, the body weight will remain constant. If,
however, the energy input is too high, some of it is

not used up in activity and this will be stored in the form of body fat. If the energy input is too low, the body starts to use up whatever store of fat it happens to have.

Different foods vary in their energy content. This is measured in calories, and foods such as butter, margarine, cream cheese, and cooking oils are extremely high in calories. Next come biscuits, cakes, sugar, dry cereals, nuts, cheese, and cream, closely followed by eggs and bread. Most fresh fruit and vegetables are fairly low in calories. Meat and fish fall in the middle section of the range, so removing them from the diet and substituting cheese and eggs makes little difference to the input side of an individual's energy equation.

But how much input do we need? First of all, energy is required to maintain the fundamental processes of life. The heart must be kept beating, the body temperature maintained, and the organs kept functioning. This requirement is called the basal metabolic rate (BMR) and is measured when a person is resting. Surprisingly, even if someone stayed in bed all day, a healthy person would still need two-thirds of their normal intake. The actual BMR varies with age and sex but the average adult needs about 1,600 calories just to cover these basic needs. However, there is considerable variation between individual rates, and people of the same sex, age, and size can differ by as much as 30%.

The BMR is constant for any particular individual but the rest of his or her energy requirements will depend on his or her activity. People doing heavy work or taking a lot of exercise need to take in more energy than those in sedentary occupations. And here again actual requirements to sustain particular activities vary by hundreds of calories. For this reason any average guidelines for energy requirements can give only a rough indication of what is needed. However, here are some examples of the total daily calorie intake that are recommended for various age groups and types of people. These figures are compiled by the Food and Nutrition Board, National Research Council:

Age	Males—calories	Females—calories
Under 1 year old	kg (weight) × 117	kg (weight) × 117
3 years old	1,300	1,300
8 years old	2,100	2,100
15 years old	3,000	3,000
19–22 years old	3,000	2,100
23–50 years old	2,700	2,000
51 and over	2,400	1,800

The trick then is to balance the energy equation, but unfortunately nothing is really known about how this is done. Some people are hearty eaters, yet they rarely put on weight. Others may get fat, not because they are excessive eaters, but because their energy expenditure is so low that they are still eating more than they are using.

The simple remedy for overweight is to eat less and exercise more. But this is easier said than done. Actually, exercise is most effective in helping to keep weight down in the first place. And remember that eating less means eating less in terms of calories. It's no good cutting out bread and potatoes only to drown your other vegetables in melted butter. Nor does eating less mean near starvation. A diet containing less than 1,400 calories probably won't contain all the nutrients required to keep the body healthy.

Food reform

Nutrition is usually taken to be concerned with maintaining health and preventing disease. However, despite the doubts of the orthodox medical profession, some doctors and nutritionists have taken the connection between food and health to its logical conclusion and have studied the effects of diet on a wide variety of diseases. As a result some of them have not only recommended specific diets to cure particular diseases, but they have achieved cures with these diets. Others have studied food allergies—an area that an increasing number of experts agree can affect the health of the individual concerned.

Some of the studies have also led to development of food reform diets for healthy people as well as for those with particular illnesses. Most of them include whole foods and many of them are vegetarian. It is not possible here to review all of them, but perhaps one of the most interesting and influential is the Bircher-Benner system developed earlier in this century by Dr. M. O. Bircher-Benner in his Swiss clinic. Among many other ideas, he is responsible for the introduction of the popular muesli (see Chapter 8, Breakfast and Brunches).

Dr. Bircher-Benner's system was developed for invalids and those poor in health through painstaking tests and clinical experience. It is designed to help them regain their fitness and vitality. This research also led to the development of a basic diet for fit people to help them avoid disease by increasing resistance and to help them combat the illnesses of old age.

It is largely, although not wholly, a vegetarian diet, avoiding meat, fish, and eggs except as accessory foods or on isolated occasions, and it cuts out all stimulating drinks such as tea, coffee, and alcohol.

Dr. Bircher-Benner came to the conclusion that the deterioration of food that takes place during cooking and other processing was at the root of many bodily evils, and his recommendations include a directive to eat at least half the daily energy intake in the form of raw food, to start each meal with raw food, and to eat green leaves every day.

Making the Most of Plant Proteins 2

Protein food has traditionally been regarded as the most important part of the diet, and in the United States this protein food has usually been meat. It takes pride of place at each meal, with the rest of the food subordinate to it. But meat is only one of the many sources of protein. The task facing the vegetarian is to choose a variety of alternative protein-rich foods that will do the same job that meat is popularly held to do so well.

Of course, much of the importance placed on protein food is justified in that it is the great body builder without which we would certainly waste away. So how much do we need and does it make any difference what kind of protein food we eat?

The protein controversy

First of all, the basic question that divides many nutritionists is "how much is enough?" This question is an extremely difficult one to answer as people vary tremendously both in their individual requirements and in their needs in different circumstances.

There are official recommended daily intake levels for all nutrients published by the Food and Nutrition Board, National Research Council. The recommended levels on these proteins take into account energy output levels. They state, for example, that the recommended daily intake of protein for a moderately active 23–50-year-old man is 56 grams (or about 2 oz), and 46 grams (about 1½ oz) for a woman of the same age. These quantities may appear to be very low, but remember that protein foods are not made up purely of protein and it may be necessary to eat more than double these amounts of protein foods to get the recommended amount of pure protein.

Following are some more recommendations from the Food and Nutrition Board:

Children	*Boys*	*Girls*
1–3 years	23 g	23 g
4–6 years	30 g	30 g
7–10 years	36 g	36 g
11–14 years	44 g	44 g
15–18 years	54 g	48 g
19–22 years	54 g	46 g
23–50 years	56 g	46 g
51 and over	56 g	46 g
Pregnant women		+30 g

However, these are "average" figures and really do not help the individual very much. They have also been adjusted upward to take into account the fact that the actual minimum protein requirements would be considered unacceptable in the United States.

The recommended daily intake of protein is worked out by plotting the results of experiments on a distribution curve. About the same number of people require less than average as require more, and the majority of people fall within 20% above and below the average. The recommended daily average is taken as the higher figure, that is, average plus 20%.

This means that there should be only a very small number of people whose needs are not met by the recommended figure. But it also means that some people could consume 40% less than the recommended figure without being deprived in any way. But there is no way of knowing where in the distribution curve a particular individual lies.

The matter is even further complicated by the fact that a person's requirements vary with the ordinary stresses and strains of everyday life. Loss of sleep, minor infections, pain, and anxiety all can cause one's protein requirement to leap by more than a third. Proteins are lost from the body even more quickly after operations, burns, and accidents, and so the body's requirement is even greater during convalescence.

Orthodox nutritionists agree that most people eating a general, mixed diet probably get more than enough protein. But some experts believe that the recommended levels are too low. They argue that to maintain vigor and youthfulness as long as possible, it is necessary to supply the body with quite large quantities of protein and that this high level should be increased to 150 grams (5½ oz) or more daily after periods of low intake or after disease. On the other hand, dieticians such as Dr. Bircher-Benner believe that 50 grams (2 oz) is nearer to the ideal daily intake.

Deficiency in protein is not easy to detect. The development of protein malnutrition is a slow and gradual process, and the first stages are quite undetectable. The issue is also complicated by the fact that the body seems to be able to adapt to lowered protein-intake levels. But whether there is any adverse long-term effect is not known.

Nor is it any good looking around to see what others are successfully eating; this will tell you nothing about your own requirements. The only answer seems to be to try and develop a kind of "body wisdom" based on the condition of your body, such as nail and hair growth, whether cuts and sores heal quickly, and how you feel in terms of energy levels and general health.

Animal or vegetable?

Meat, usually thought to be the great protein provider, is not in fact the richest source of protein. It ranks somewhere in the middle of the percentage quantity scale, with around 25% protein in its makeup. Soya

flour is actually the most concentrated natural source
of protein, containing almost half its weight in protein.
Next come certain cheeses such as Parmesan, which is
36% protein. Meat follows, with fish, nuts, beans,
peas, and lentils in the same category. At the lower
end of the scale are the cereals and eggs, at around
10%, and milk at about 4%, although dried skimmed
milk contains 34% protein. Vegetables are also near
the bottom of the scale.

However, it is not just the quantity of protein
contained in food that decides how useful it will be in
body building. If it were, vegans and vegetarians
would not need to be concerned about protein levels
and there would be no controversy about preferable
protein sources. After all, most dairy produce and
many plant proteins have an excellent showing on the
quantity scale.

However, all proteins are not the same. The protein
in milk differs from that in cereals and the protein in
liver is different to that in soya beans. But all of them
are made up of a combination of the same twenty-two
amino acids. These amino acids are released into the
bloodstream during digestion, and they are carried to
wherever they are needed to be reassembled into body
proteins.

Some amino acids are produced naturally in the
body. But eight of them are not, and for the building
of new body proteins to continue these eight essential
amino acids must be provided from proteins eaten in
the daily diet. In addition, they need to be present
simultaneously and in the right proportions, otherwise
protein synthesis will fall to a very low level. The other
amino acids in foods are also used in body building,
but they are not considered essential as the body can,
if necessary, manufacture them for itself.

All the essential amino acids are present in most
foods, but unfortunately they do not necessarily occur
in the ideal proportions for the body to use. There are
usually one or more amino acids present in dispropor-
tionately small quantities. This means that if half the

ideal proportions of one of the essential amino acids is missing from a protein, the body can only use half the total quantity of all the other essential amino acids present. The rest is wasted or used to supply energy. It also means that twice the amount of that protein would need to be eaten to fulfill daily requirements. The most deficient amino acid is called the limiting amino acid.

The highest quality proteins would be those in which there was no limiting amino acid and all the protein was usable by the body. In practice the total amount of protein eaten is never fully usable by the body, but the protein in eggs comes very near to it. In fact, animal proteins occupy the highest rungs on the usability scale and for this reason they used to be listed as first-class proteins. However, meat is not at the top; milk, cheese, and fish are all higher up the scale.

Some vegetable proteins approach the level of meat and these include soya beans and whole rice. The rest of the nuts and beans are in the 40–60% usability range, and this, of course, means that it would be necessary to eat rather a lot of them to cover daily requirements because of the limiting amino acids waste. This is an important consideration in a vegan diet.

For vegetarians the situation is very much easier. Dairy produce is high on the usability scale, and some of them—dried skim milk and Parmesan cheese, for example—are also high on the percentage quantity scale. Contrary to popular belief, it doesn't look as if vegetarians are likely to miss out in the protein stakes.

Complementary proteins

However, it would be a pity to dismiss plant proteins out of hand—they are cheap and plentiful and add great variety to the diet. The trick is to eat proteins that have mutually complementary amino acid patterns, that is, one protein that is low in one particular amino acid is matched with a protein that is rich in the same amino acid. In this way the protein value of the meal is increased in such a way that the whole is greater than the sum of the parts. This is because the matching of amino acids means that more of each protein is available for use by the body. Such protein mixes do not result in a perfect protein, but they can increase the protein quantity by as much as 50% above the average of the items eaten separately.

Many people unconsciously take advantage of this complementary effect. Bread and cheese, for example, complement each other very well, the cheese filling in the bread's lysine and isoleucine deficiencies. Baked beans on toast is another example. Here the combination of wheat and beans can increase the amount of usable protein by up to 33%.

So what are the most effective combinations?

1) Milk products and grains
Dairy products have excellent usability ratings and they thus make good supplements to any foods. But they are particularly rich in two amino acids and, as we saw with the bread and cheese example, combine particularly well with cereals that are low in the same two amino acids.

You don't need to add much of the milk product to increase the protein quality quite substantially. Two tablespoons of nonfat dried milk, for example, added to 100 g (4 oz) wheat or rye flour increase the protein quality by about 45%.

The same amino acid strengths mean that dairy products also complement the proteins in nuts and seeds. So that cheese and peanuts or milk and sesame seeds make good combinations.

2) Pulses (beans, peas, lentils) and grains
The proteins in pulses and grains have almost exactly opposite strengths and weaknesses, and therefore complement each other well. The addition of milk can add even more to the protein quality of these combinations.

3) Pulses and seeds

A similar situation occurs with the amino acids of pulses and nuts and seeds. Once again dairy produce can help to fill the amino acid gaps in nuts and seeds, and a good mixture is peanut butter with milk for sauces.

Much more detailed information on complementary proteins and the proportion in which they should be mixed is given in *Diet for a Small Planet* by Frances Moore Lappe (see Bibliography).

Here is a guide to the amount of usable protein in average servings of some of the various protein foods eaten by vegetarians.

Food		Total Weight	Total Grams of Protein	Weight of Usable Protein
Dairy Produce				
Cottage cheese		100 g	17 g	13 g
Milk nonfat dry solids		25 g	10 g	8 g
Parmesan cheese		25 g	10 g	
Milk		100 g	9 g	7 g
Yogurt		100 g	8 g	7 g
Cheddar cheese		25 g	7 g	7 g
Edam cheese		25 g	8 g	7 g
Pulses				
Add 5% if complemented				
Soya beans	(dry)	50 g	17 g	10 g
Broad beans	(dry)	50 g	13 g	6 g
Kidney beans	(dry)	50 g	12 g	5 g
Chick peas	(dry)	50 g	11 g	5 g
Lentils	(dry)	50 g	13 g	4 g
Nuts and Seeds				
Add 2-3% if complemented				
Sunflower seeds		25 g	7 g	4 g
Peanuts		25 g	8 g	3 g
Cashew nuts		25 g	5 g	3 g
Sesame seeds		25 g	5 g	3 g

Grains and Their Products
Add 2–3% if complemented

Pasta	150 g	5 g	3 g
Oatmeal	50 g	4 g	3 g
Brown rice	75 g	5 g	3 g
Wheat germ	12 g	3 g	2 g
Bread, whole wheat	1 slice	2.4 g	1.2 g
Soya bean flour defatted	138 g	65 g	40 g
Soya bean flour full fat	138 g	52 g	32 g
Whole wheat flour	120 g	16 g	10 g

A final point to note is that all protein whether of high or low quality is only used efficiently if there is sufficient energy in the diet. Theoretically the daily requirement of protein could be supplied by six eggs. But if these were eaten alone, the low energy/calorie content would mean that most of the amino acids would be diverted away from repair work to supply energy. This means that high protein diets should be looked at with care as they may not be doing the job they are designed to do.

On the other hand, most protein foods contain fats and carbohydrates as well as protein in their makeup and this will affect their calorie contribution to the body's energy balance. It does not mean, however, that such protein foods are necessarily fattening. Cheese, for example, has a high fat content, but because the protein in cheese is of such a high quality only small quantities are required to fulfill daily requirements. Nuts, on the other hand, do have very high calorie to usable protein ratios. Incidentally, one of the least fattening high protein foods is cottage cheese, closely followed by skim milk and buttermilk.

Planning Balanced Menus 3

Planning balanced menus involves selecting the right balance of different types of food to build up and maintain good health. But it also involves selecting food that tastes delicious and looks attractive. There is no point in producing an extremely healthy meal if it looks unattractive and unappetizing. The digestive juices will not work so well and your family or friends could be put off the idea of healthy foods permanently.

Nor will they want to eat the same things—however nutritious—day in and day out. Variety is extremely important, and here the judicious use of fresh foods in season, the freezer, and your imagination can help to bring changes.

Planning the day for a balanced diet

Ideally, each meal in the day should contain some of all the essential nutrients, and certainly they should all appear at some time during the day. This is because many of them are not stored in the body and therefore need to be supplied regularly. In addition, if protein is not eaten with an energy source, it will be used to provide energy rather than to rebuild the body tissues.

Few foods are made up of only one nutrient and conversely no food contains all the nutrients we need. But of course we don't really think of eating nutrients—

26

it is food that we enjoy at mealtimes. Perhaps the easiest way to plan a balanced diet is to divide food into categories according to major attributes and then to choose something from each group for each meal. Below are four groups of food selected as especially good sources of particular nutrients.

1) Eggs, cheese, milk, pulses (beans, peas, lentils), and nuts:
   supply protein, B group vitamins, vitamins A and D, and minerals.
2) Bread, cereals, rice and pasta:
   supply carbohydrates for energy, Vitamin E, minerals, and fiber; can also add to the protein supply.
3) Cooking and salad oil, butter, cream, margarine:
   supply fats for longer term energy and vitamins A and D.
4) Fruit and vegetables:
   supply vitamins A, B group, and C, minerals, and fiber.

The traditional pattern of breakfast, lunch, and dinner probably fulfills the nutritional requirements as well as any although there is some disagreement about the relative weight of the various meals. Some experts would have you eat like royalty at breakfast, lesser royalty at midday, and a pauper in the evening. Others suggest a light breakfast and supper, with the main meal of the day at midday.

However, this is not a convenient pattern for everyone, and some people are forced to or wish to eat their main meal in the evening. This should not cause too many problems so long as the meal is not eaten so late that the digestive process interferes with sleep patterns and provided that a good breakfast is eaten before going to work.

Unfortunately, many people start the day on a hastily consumed cup of coffee or tea and maybe a piece of toast or some cereal. Others do without breakfast altogether. Yet breakfast really is an essential start

to the day. Many authorities believe that breakfast
should provide at least a quarter of your daily food
intake. After all, breakfast usually follows a fast of
anything up to twelve hours and that is far longer than
any other gap between meals in the twenty-four hour
cycle.

First thing in the morning, the body's blood sugar
level is at its lowest, and breakfast provides the essential nutrients when they are needed most. It is the
amount of sugar in your blood that determines the
amount of energy you can produce, and this in turn
affects how you think and act throughout the day.
Studies in the United States show that the omission of
breakfast results in poorer scholastic performance in
schoolchildren and in higher accident rates for factory
workers and truck drivers.

Dieters are major offenders when it comes to skip-
ping breakfast as this seems an easy way of cutting
down on overall food intake. But this can lead to
cheating because of hunger at midmorning or overeat-
ing at lunch. It is actually far better to eat small meals
at regular intervals throughout the day.

Planning individual meals

As well as fulfilling nutritional and health requirements, a meal should be an enjoyable pastime, and
there are a number of simple factors that can really
make a difference to the appeal and taste of a meal.

The first of these is the choice of flavorings to be
used. This is a particularly important consideration for
vegetarian food, which too often tends to be insipid or
bland. Of course, nuts, pulses, and cereals do have a
flavor of their own, but these can often be greatly
enhanced by the careful choice of flavorings. So it is
important to experiment with flavorings. But don't go
mad on the latest discovery and use it in every dish.
The same herb or spice in the main dish or sauce
would become extremely monotonous.

Texture, too, is important. It is not good dietetically, nor does it make an interesting meal, if there is more than one dish prepared and finished in the same way. Several dishes made with pastry or deep-fried would be boring. So it is best to vary the textures by serving crunchy vegetables with light soufflés and smooth dishes, a creamy sauce with pastry dishes, and rice or potatoes with casseroles.

The look of the food can also set the taste buds working. So mix colors as well as textures and avoid food that is all white or all brown. Arrange the food attractively on serving dishes or individual plates and use garnishes to improve its appearance. Parsley, crumbled egg yolk, tomatoes, watercress, and roasted nuts are all effective, and you can easily experiment with other things.

In the United States, we are generally used to three-course meals with a main course consisting of a principal dish with vegetables. However, the emphasis can shift a little with vegetarian meals. Sometimes the dishes will all have equal weight. But do make sure there are not too many rich or fatty dishes in the same meal. This can be both overwhelming and bad for the digestion.

One final point concerns the balance of raw and cooked foods. To some extent this will depend on your own inclinations and convictions. But it is a fact that fresh raw food often contains more of its original nutrients. This is because some vitamins are destroyed by heat and others are leached out into the cooking liquid, and this is often thrown away.

Dr. Bircher-Benner suggested that a raw food dish should be used to start every meal, and this is a convenient method of making sure that you have a regular intake of raw foods. Other people like to eat at least one raw food or salad meal each day. But whatever style of eating you choose, do make sure that you don't overcook your food—particularly vegetables—and that

you don't leave chopped or grated raw food exposed
to the air; both are sure ways of losing much of their
goodness.

Making the most
of complementary proteins

Perhaps the most important thing to remember when
using plant proteins is that your daily protein requirement need not necessarily come from one large important item in the two main meals of the day. In fact, it
is much more likely that it will come from the sum
total of all the protein-containing foods eaten during
the day.

It is an easy step from the realization of this fact to
making a conscious effort to enhance the protein value
of particular dishes either by adding extra protein-rich
ingredients or by making use of the complementary
protein theory.

The three most effective combinations of protein
foods, outlined in Chapter 2, are milk products and
grains, pulses and grains, and pulses and seeds. Below
are some good examples of these combinations and
some hints on putting them into practice.

Milk products and grains
Cereals with milk: *muesli* (see chapter 8)

Bread and cheese: *sandwiches*

Cheese and rice: *rissoles and patties*

Milk, cheese, and cornmeal: *polenta*

Milk and wheat flour: *sauces*

Cheese and pasta: *baked casseroles*

Try adding milk, cream, or yogurt to potato dishes. The
greater the amount of milk product, the better the overall
protein value.

Use nonfat dried milk with grains and pulses. Don't
bother to dilute it—just add it in its dry state.

Pulses and grains

Beans and wheat flour or bread: *baked beans on toast*

Peas and beans with rice: *risotto*

Beans and corn: *vegetable casseroles*

When using pulses and rice, the best combination from a complementary protein point of view is about 3:1 grains to pulses. If the recipe calls for a higher ratio of beans, add some milk products or seeds.

Use soya flour in cakes and pastries to give a nice short texture as well as to increase the protein content. Soya flour can also be added to bread and pancakes. Use to replace flour on a 7:1 ratio.

Add soya flour to pâtés, terrines (casseroles), and rissoles.

Pulses and seeds

Chick peas and sesame seeds: *Houmous*

Beans and nuts: *terrines and pâtés*

Beans and sunflower seeds: *vegetable stuffings*

All bean dishes are enhanced proteinwise by the addition of a milk product. Serve butter beans in white sauce or red beans with cottage cheese and herbs.

Add nuts and seeds to salads and to vegetable dishes.

Add protein to desserts by including soya flour or ground nuts in crunchy toppings and in pastry.

Ingredients and Basic Preparation 4

The majority of ingredients used in the menus and recipe sections are to be found in most large supermarkets and much of it is everyday produce on sale all over the country. Even foreign vegetables can be bought in most towns today, and other vegetables are fairly easy to come by in season and nearly always available frozen.

A few items such as buckwheat, fennel, and sesame seed and some of the more exotic beans will require a visit to a specialist market or to the local health food store. And it is probably sensible to stock up on things like canned chestnuts, artichoke hearts, and flageolet (green kidney beans) when you happen to see them.

With the cereals, my own inclination is for wholewheat flour and pasta, brown rice, and the like. Many of these are now available in ordinary stores and supermarkets, so it isn't necessary to do all your shopping at the health food shop unless you want to.

Herbs and spices are particularly important in vegetarian cookery, so stock up on them. If you have a garden, grow as wide a variety as you can. Use them fresh in summer and dry them for the winter months.

Basic equipment

There is a common misconception that vegetarian cookery takes ages to prepare—all that chopping and grinding! But this isn't really the case. However, all

32

good cooking takes some time to prepare, so a careful selection of useful equipment can help to cut down preparation time.

The vegetarian cook doesn't really need much in the way of extra equipment, although a mechanical or electric grater is a big help if you are keen on salads and a pressure cooker dramatically cuts the time that beans take to cook. So plan your kitchen in the normal way, adding some of the items listed below depending on the type of food you like to prepare and the size of your budget.

> French cook's knife—your basic tool for most dishes
> Mechanical or electric grater
> Blender/liquidizer with grinder attachment
> Mouli-mill for soups and purées—gives a coarser texture than the liquidizer
> Pressure cooker
> Double boiler
> Two or three stainless steel steamers to fit inside your pans
> Wire whisk for sauces

A good set of pans is really worth investing in. Go for stainless steel—with a copper base if you can afford it. Alternatively enameled cast iron is fine, although you should get rid of it if it chips. Many people believe that aluminum is dangerous and copper kills any vitamin C that remains during cooking. A thick base spreads the heat—particularly important for top-of-the-stove cookery.

Some recipes suggest that the dish is cooked "au bain marie." The simplest way to do this is to fill a roasting pan with about 5 cm (2 in) water and place the dish to be cooked in this.

The store cupboard

A store (or well-stocked) cupboard is always useful, and this is particularly true for the vegetarian cook. Some items require advance cooking. It's no good rushing out to buy blackeye beans, for example, the day you want to eat them; unless you have a pressure cooker they won't be ready until the next day. Other items such as herbs and spices are in constant demand and need to be on hand.

Here is a checklist of most of the items I keep in my own store cupboard.

Herbs
Thyme, marjoram, basil, sage, summer savory, rosemary, tarragon, chives, dill weed, chervil, oregano, bay leaves, mint, parsley, fennel and dill seed, celery seed, and celery salt.

Spices
Allspice, ground cumin seed, caraway seeds, turmeric, cardamoms, coriander, cloves; ground, root, and stem ginger; nutmeg and mace, cinnamon, curry powder, mixed spices; black, white, Cayenne, and paprika pepper; sea salt.

Flavorings and Sauces
Vanilla and almond essence, garlic and garlic salt, tomato paste, Marmite or Barmene, French and English mustard, Worcestershire sauce (not for strict vegetarians), cider and wine vinegar, and tomato ketchup.

Nuts, Pulses, and Seeds
Peanuts, almonds, walnuts, cashew nuts, hazelnuts, peanut butter, sesame seeds, soya flour, lentils, and a selection of dried peas and beans.

Cereals
Plain and self-raising flour, fine and medium oatmeal, rolled oats, buckwheat, flaked barley, flaked millet, muesli mix, yellow cornmeal, rice, and a selection of pasta.

Preserves and Sweeteners
Homemade jams, chutneys, and pickles, honey, molasses, Barbados sugar, demerara sugar, a little caster sugar for special desserts, and a selection of dried fruits.

Miscellaneous
> Baking powder, cream of tartar, bicarbonate of soda, agar-agar, gelozone, nonfat dried milk powder, and a selection of canned foods for standbys and luxuries.

Cheese
> For really strict vegetarians, it is probably worth noting that cheeses made with vegetarian rennet are available at most health food stores and some supermarkets.

Apart from canned foods, avoid buying too much of any one item unless you are really sure you will get through it quickly. There is nothing worse than looking at a mountain of beans or spaghetti and wondering if you will ever come to the end of it. These items do deteriorate overtime so they are best eaten fresh.

Basic preparation

Some of the items used in the recipes could be unfamiliar. So here is a rundown on basic preparation.

1) Pulses

In general, dried pulses need to be soaked before cooking. This can be done overnight in cold water. Alternatively the process can be speeded up by pouring boiling water over the dried pulses and leaving them to stand for about 2 hours before cooking. However, this method does tend to split the skins.

> *Lentils:* No soaking required. Simmer for about 30–45 minutes depending on how "mushy" you like them.
>
> *Split peas:* No soaking required. Simmer for about 1 hour.
>
> *Pinto beans, Borlotti beans, red kidney beans, and Greek Foulia beans:* Soak overnight in cold water. Simmer for about 1 hour then start to check the softness of the beans. If they are left too long, they will start to fall.
>
> *Chick peas, whole green peas, haricot beans, blackeye beans, and butter beans:* Soak overnight in cold water. Simmer for about 1½ hours and then start checking.

Soya beans: Soak overnight in the refrigerator. Soya beans tend to start fermenting if left in a warm kitchen. Simmer for at least 2 hours. Even when fully cooked, soya beans tend to retain a slight "bite."

Always add salt at the end of cooking as salt seems to make the beans harder to soften. Some people add a pinch of bicarbonate of soda to speed up the cooking time of beans. But this shortcut should be used sparingly.

The pressure cooker will at least halve the amount of time required to cook beans. Use plenty of water and experiment to find ideal times.

2) Whole meal flour

All recipes have been tested with whole meal flour, but they all work just as well with white flour. I do not find that there is usually any need to change the proportion of ingredients when using whole meal flour in place of white flour. However, some people prefer to use 80% extraction flour for cakes and pastry as this gives a smoother texture. The degree to which the flour has been milled will also affect the texture of the finished dish.

Here are pointers to bear in mind when using whole meal flour:

Pastry made with whole meal flour tends to be extremely crumbly and can be difficult to roll out. This can be overcome either by adding a little more water than usual or by pressing the pastry into the pie dish without rolling it out. The latter method is particularly useful for sugar pastry made with whole meal flour.

Sauces made with whole meal flour look a little speckled. This is due to the bran in the flour and this can be sieved out if preferred. A roux sauce is made by melting butter over a low heat and stirring in the flour. Cook the mixture for 2–3 minutes and then gradually add the liquid, stirring all the time. Bring to boil and cook for a few minutes. A panada is a particularly thick roux sauce.

Whole wheat pasta behaves in almost exactly the same

way as white pasta, and ravioli dough made with whole meal flour rolls out extremely well.

3) Polenta

Use a wire whisk when adding cornmeal to boiling water. This helps to prevent lumps forming. If the mixture does go lumpy, just pass through a sieve and continue as instructed. This note also applies to semolina and rice flour recipes.

4) Brown rice

All the recipes in this book have been tested with brown rice. This takes a little longer to cook than polished rice and has a nutty flavor. It does not need to be washed after cooking as the grains remain separate.

5) Sesame seeds

Unless they are being used for decoration, sesame seeds are usually ground before use. They are thought to be much more digestible used in this way. To toast them, sprinkle whole sesame seeds into the base of the grill pan and place under the heat for 2–3 minutes until brown in color. Do not allow them to burn. Grind and store in an airtight jar.

6) Nuts

Nuts are usually cheaper if bought whole in their brown skins, and these are usually removed before use. To remove skin, shake peanuts in a bag, rubbing slightly at the same time. Hazelnuts will need 5 minutes in the oven before shaking or rubbing the skins loose. Almonds should be placed in a pan of boiling water for 1 minute or so, after which the skins are easily removed.

7) Dried fruits

Raisins, currants, dates, and sultanas are used as bought. Dried bananas can be used soaked or unsoaked. Dried apricots, prunes, peaches, apples, and

pears need soaking overnight in cold water. Wash the
fruit first and then use the water in which the fruit has
been soaked to cook them.

8) Dairy produce
I have used butter for testing all the recipes, but there
is no reason why a good margarine should not be used
instead.

9) Vegetarian stock
There are three types of stock available to the vegetarian, and the choice will depend on the strength and
flavor required for the particular recipe. They are made
as follows:

> Vegetable water saved from simmering, steaming, or
> baking vegetables. This can be kept for a few days in
> the refrigerator or stored for longer periods in the freez-
> er. Try freezing some in ice trays; the cubes can then be
> stored in polythene bags in the freezer and small quan-
> tities used for baking more vegetables or for sauces.
>
> Specially prepared strong stock can be made by boiling
> one large sliced onion, one sliced carrot, a stick of celery,
> bay leaf and parsley and thyme in a pint of water for
> about 1 hour. Strain and use or store.
>
> A vegetable extract such as Marmite or Barmene dis-
> solved in water makes an excellent standby stock, or the
> extract can be added to the stocks above to give added
> color and strength.

10) Setting agents
Gelatine is, of course, of animal origin and strict
vegetarians will not want to use it. However, if you do
use it remember to mix with a little cold water first
before adding hot water to dissolve it. The gelatine
should not be boiled.

Agar-agar is one vegetarian alternative. It gives a
really clear jelly and is made by sprinkling into boiling
liquid and stirring vigorously until completely dissolved. Particular care is needed to make sure it does

not go lumpy. If it does, it can be strained. Agar-agar starts to set very quickly after removing from the heat, so use at once.

Gelozone is another vegetarian alternative to gelatine. It must always be made into a smooth paste with cold water and then brought to the boil and simmered for 2–3 minutes.

11) Bean sprouts

Bean sprouts are on sale in a number of stores, but it is a very simple matter to sprout your own. Sprouting at home also means that you have a much wider choice of sprouts—some seed houses offer as many as a dozen different varieties.

The choice ranges from the mung bean of the familiar Chinese beanshoot, to alfalfa seed and spicey fenugreek, to special mixtures devised by the seed sellers. Don't try to sprout beans that have been sitting around your store cupboard for the last 6 months.

Sprouts are particularly rich in protein as well as in essential vitamins and minerals. They also contain dietary fiber and a number of enzymes that help in digestion. They are about the freshest vegetable you are ever likely to have as they are still growing when you eat them. Even fresh garden vegetables lose 25% of their vitamins within 30 minutes of being picked.

Sprouting is extremely easy. All you need to do is to place a small amount of the seed or beans in a large jar and cover the neck with a piece of muslin or gauze. Next fill the container with tepid water and shake well to clean the seed. Repeat this 3 times and then leave the container on its side so that the water will drain away.

Fill the jar with more tepid water every morning and every evening for about 4–6 days, making sure that the water can drain away easily. Don't let the sprouts grow too big or they will lose their flavor and nutritional value.

Sprouts are best eaten raw, but they can be lightly steamed or sautéed. But do make sure not to overcook them. Excess sprouts store well in the refrigerator in a covered plastic container.

Freezing vegetarian food

The freezer is just as useful to the vegetarian cook as it is to the general cook. The way you use it will, of course, depend on your life-style and on the kind of food that you and your family prefer. However, there are some things that are extremely convenient to have readily available in the refrigerator. These include:

Cooked rice	Batter and pancake mixes
Cooked beans	Bread and rolls
Grated cheese	Basic sauces
Bread crumbs	Fresh herbs
Pastry	Grated orange and lemon rind
Fruit purées	Stock

It's a good idea to freeze vegetable stock in ice-cube containers and then store in plastic bags. This means that you can use as little or as much stock as you require.

Remember, too, that some things do not freeze well. These include eggs in their shells, hard-boiled eggs in any form, mayonnaise, and nutmeg. Most spices take on a rather more peppery or ginger flavor, and vanilla can develop a very unpleasant taste if kept frozen for too long. Curry, too, gets stronger after a while and most sauces tend to thicken up. Mashed potato freezes well, but sliced or cubed potatoes in soups and stews tend to fall, making the finished dish rather cloudy. It is, therefore, probably better to add the potatoes when the dish has been reheated prior to serving.

Textured vegetable protein

Textured vegetable protein (TVP) is now available in a variety of forms, ranging from plain, unflavored chunks, slices, and mince to canned varieties, emulating the classic dishes of English, French, and Italian cuisine. Most of it is based on soya beans.

TVP is very much a matter of personal taste. It can be very economical and is nutritionally excellent. However, I prefer my beans to look and taste like beans and so I have not included any recipes for TVP.

Using dietary supplements

Here again we are back into the realms of controversy. Most orthodox nutritionists state that dietary supplements are not really necessary for most Americans as our diet is sufficiently varied. Other experts believe that the modern diet is lacking in various elements and that these deficiencies should be made good by the addition of items such as wheat germ and brewers' yeast and vitamins. Certainly natural supplements such as these are unlikely to do you any harm and they could be extremely valuable. The trouble is that on the whole they are not very palatable, although enthusiasts state that you gradually get used to the flavor. However, quite often they can be mixed in with other ingredients to mask the flavor. Items to consider are:

1) Brewers' yeast powder
This is rich in vitamins of the B complex as well as having relatively high protein content. One level tablespoon will provide 2 grams of usable protein, or around 5% of your total daily requirements. The amino acid pattern also makes it a good complementary mix for nuts and cereals.

2) Wheat germ
This has a similar protein content to brewers' yeast and is rich in vitamin E, but its general level of vitamins and minerals is not nearly as good.

3) Wheat bran
This can be added to soups and cereals to improve the fiber content of the diet.

The Main Meal 5
of the Day

menu

Stuffed Onions with Rosemary
Potato Stew with Spiced Red Cabbage
and Green Beans
Bananas in Honey

Stuffed Onions
with Rosemary

Steam onions and allow to cool slightly. Remove centers from onions and chop finely. Mix with ground beans, rosemary, and seasoning. Spoon back into the centers of the onions. Place onions on a heatproof plate and dot with butter. Place under the grill and cook for 5–8 minutes until well browned.

4 large or 8 small onions
100 g (4 oz) ground
   cooked soya beans
1 teaspoon rosemary
salt and pepper

Potato Stew

Finely slice onions and fry in cooking oil until golden. Add oatmeal and continue cooking for a few minutes. Then add stock and Marmite. Bring to boil, stirring from time to time and add chopped potatoes and seasoning. Simmer for 30 minutes until potatoes are cooked, adding a little more stock if the stew gets too thick. Serve sprinkled with a little grated cheese if desired.

4 large potatoes
4 onions
4 tablespoons fine or
   medium oatmeal
1 tablespoon Marmite or
   yeast extract
625 ml (1¼ pints)
   vegetable stock
cooking oil
salt and pepper
grated cheese (optional)

Spiced Red Cabbage

Slice red cabbage and place in a thick-based pan. Mix stock, vinegar, and Worcestershire sauce. Add spices and seasoning and pour over the cabbage. Bring to boil and simmer for 45 minutes or until cabbage is soft.

1 small red cabbage
15 ml (1 tablespoon)
   vinegar
45 ml (3 tablespoons)
   stock
2 cloves
5 ml (1 teaspoon)
   Worcestershire sauce
¼ teaspoon cinnamon
¼ teaspoon nutmeg
salt and pepper

Bananas in Honey

Melt butter in a frying pan. Add honey and lemon juice. Quickly sauté peeled and halved bananas in this mixture. Serve with remaining liquid poured over the top.

4 bananas
2 tablespoons honey
juice of 1 lemon
knob of butter

Cream of Leek Soup
Fennel Bean Pot with Potato Cakes
and Endive Salad with Onion Dressing
Orange Slices with Pears

Cream of Leek Soup

Melt butter in pan and add chopped onion. Sauté until golden. Add chopped leeks and continue to cook for 3–4 minutes. Add cooking sherry and bring to boil. Add all other ingredients and bring to boil again. Simmer for 45 minutes and rub through a sieve or mouli. Correct seasoning and reheat. Garnish with heads of mustard and cress.

450 g (1 lb) leeks
1 tablespoon English
   mustard powder
1 medium onion
25 g (1 oz) butter
75 ml (3 fl.oz) cooking
   sherry
625 ml (1¼ pints)
   vegetable stock
½ teaspoon sugar
salt and pepper

Garnish
mustard and cress

Fennel Bean Pot

Soak beans overnight. Finely slice onions and garlic and fry in a little cooking oil until golden. Add beans and mix with fennel seed, chervil, and seasoning. Transfer to an earthenware casserole dish and pour on red wine. Cover and bake at 190°C/375°F for 1½ hours. Increase temperature to 200°C/400°F for a further 40–45 minutes. Stir from time to time.

50 g (2 oz) haricot beans
50 g (2 oz) blackeye
   beans
50 g (2 oz) butter beans
50 g (2 oz) Borlotti beans
2 onions
2 cloves garlic
250 ml (½ pint) red wine
½ teaspoon fennel seed
½ teaspoon chervil or
   parsley
cooking oil
salt and pepper

44

Potato Cakes

Peel and boil potatoes until soft. Mash with butter and milk and mix in flour and seasoning. Press out on a greased baking tray to about ¼ in thick. Mark into sections with a knife. Bake at 200°C/400°F for 40–45 minutes until slightly crisp and brown. Serve with butter.

450 g (1 lb) potatoes
4 tablespoons plain flour
50 g (2 oz) butter or
  margarine
45 ml (3 tablespoons)
  milk or stock
salt and pepper

Endive Salad
with Onion Dressing

Wash curly endive and tear into pieces. Mix with thinly cut slices of red and green pepper. Mix dressing ingredients with finely chopped onions and pour over salad. Serve at once.

½ head curly endive
¼ green pepper
¼ red pepper

Dressing
60 ml (4 tablespoons)
  salad oil
30 ml (2 tablespoons)
  cider vinegar
4 spring onions or ¼
  small onion
black pepper

Sliced Oranges
with Pears

Peel and slice pears and oranges and arrange alternately in a dish. Squeeze third orange and pour the juice over the fruit. Chill and serve with whipped cream.

2 oranges
2 pears
juice of 1 orange

Guernsey Salad
Dutch Pea Soup with Nut Dumplings
Apples Stuffed with Raisins and Honey

Guernsey Salad

Skin the tomatoes and roughly chop. Mix sour cream, lemon juice, seasoning, and mint. Arrange tomatoes in individual dishes on a bed of lettuce. Spoon the dressing over the top.

8 tomatoes
45 ml (3 tablespoons) sour cream
10 ml (2 teaspoons) lemon juice
1 tablespoon freshly chopped mint
salt and pepper
lettuce

Dutch Pea Soup

Soak peas overnight in water. Drain and make the liquid up to 1 liter (2 pints) with more water. Slice onions and brown in cooking oil. Add peas, water, Marmite, and a sprinkling of nutmeg. Season and bring to boil. Simmer for about 1½ hours. Purée and serve with nut dumplings.

225 g (8 oz) split green peas
2 large onions
1 teaspoon Marmite or yeast extract
sprinkling of nutmeg
salt and pepper
water
cooking oil

Nut Dumplings

Soak bread crumbs in milk. Add the peanuts and egg and beat well. If the mixture is too runny to form into balls, add flour to make a stiffish paste. Season and shape into 20 small dumplings about 1 cm (½ in) in diameter. Drop into soup or into boiling salted water and cook for 5–8 minutes. Serve with soup.

25 g (1 oz) bread crumbs
25 g (1 oz) ground peanuts
30 ml (2 tablespoons) milk
1 egg
a little self-raising flour
salt and pepper

Apples Stuffed with Raisins and Honey

Wash and core apples and cut round the center to stop the skin splitting. Dust raisins with cinnamon and stuff into the center of the apples. Top with a teaspoon of honey on each apple. Bake in a fairly hot oven for about 45 minutes–1 hour, 200°C/400°F.

4 cooking apples
4 tablespoons raisins
4 teaspoons honey
1 teaspoon cinnamon

menu

Grapefruit and Orange Salad
**Polenta Tomato Casserole with Jacket Potatoes
and Baked Leeks**
Apple Crunchy Pudding with Custard

Grapefruit and Orange Salad

Peel and slice 2 grapefruit and 1 orange and divide into 4 bowls. Squeeze the remaining orange and pour over the fruit. Chop the sprigs of mint and sprinkle over the top and place an olive in the center of each dish. Serve chilled.

2 grapefruit
2 oranges
4 sprigs mint
4 black olives

Polenta Tomato Casserole

Bring water to boil and pour in cornmeal, stirring all the time. Add salt and butter and continue stirring until mixture thickens. Continue cooking on a low heat for 20–30 minutes, stirring regularly. The finished mixture should be thick and smooth. Add Parmesan and nutmeg and correct seasoning. Pour into a basin and allow to cool and set. Meanwhile make a roux sauce with the remaining butter, flour, and milk and season to taste. Slice cold polenta into thin wedges and layer in a casserole dish with finely sliced onions and tomatoes. Sprinkle with remaining Parmesan and top with sauce. Finish off with bread crumbs and a little more nutmeg. Bake in a moderate oven 190°C/375°F for 30–40 minutes.

Polenta
10 g (4 oz) yellow cornmeal
750 ml (1½ pints) water
50 g (2 oz) butter
50 g (2 oz) Parmesan cheese
½ teaspoon salt
¼ teaspoon nutmeg

Sauce
50 g (2 oz) butter
50 g (2 oz) flour
375 ml (⅔ pint) milk
salt and pepper

Other Ingredients
3 onions
4 large tomatoes
50 g (2 oz) Parmesan cheese
25 g (1 oz) bread crumbs

Baked Leeks

Wash and slice leeks and layer in a casserole with frozen peas. Add herbs and seasoning and cover. Bake in a moderate oven 190°C/375°F for 1 hour.

4 medium leeks
4 tablespoons frozen peas
a little rosemary
salt and pepper

Apple Crunchy Pudding

Peel and slice apples. Simmer with a very little water and purée. Place in the base of an ovenproof dish. Mix Demerara sugar and bran flakes and sprinkle on the top of the apple purée. Bake at 200°C/400°F for 30 minutes.

700 g (1½ lb) cooking apples
25 g (1 oz) Demerara sugar
25 g (1 oz) bran flakes
a little water

Tomato, Cauliflower, and Tarragon Soup
with Whole Meal Rolls
South American Baked Eggs
with Steamed Broccoli and Vichy Carrots
Pear and Ginger Crumble Pudding

Tomato, Cauliflower and Tarragon Soup

Melt butter in pan and add chopped onion. Sauté until golden. Add cooking sherry and bring to boil. Add cauliflower, tomatoes, vegetable stock, sugar, tarragon, and seasoning. Bring to boil and simmer 45 minutes. Rub through sieve or mouli. Correct seasoning and reheat. Serve sprinkled with a little more tarragon.

225 g (8 oz) cauliflower
225 g (8 oz) tomatoes
1 medium onion
1 oz butter
75 ml (3 fl.oz) cooking
   sherry
625 ml (1¼ pints)
vegetable stock
1 teaspoon dried tarragon
½ teaspoon sugar
salt and pepper

Whole Meal Rolls

Warm water to blood heat and mix 3–4 tablespoons with the dried yeast. Leave in a warm place for about 10 minutes until creamy. Sift flour and salt and keep in a warm place. Mix flour, water, and yeast mixture and knead in the bowl for 5–10 minutes. Shape into rolls and place on a greased baking tray. Cover with a cloth and leave in a warm place to rise to double their size (about 1 hour). Bake in a hot oven 230°C/450°F for 10–12 minutes. Test if the rolls are ready by rapping the base with your fingernails. It should sound firm.

450 g (1 lb) whole meal
   flour
325–350 ml (13–14 fl.oz)
   warm water
1 teaspoon salt
12 g (½ oz) dried yeast

South American Baked Eggs

Finely chop onions and green pepper and fry in cooking oil until the onions are transparent. Mash beans with a fork and mix with onion mixture. Add thyme and seasoning and spoon into an ovenproof dish. Make four wells in the mixture and break an egg into each one. Pour over the wine and bake at 220°C/425°F for about 15–20 minutes or until the eggs are set.

4 onions
1 green pepper
325 g (12 oz) cooked red beans
4 large eggs
60 ml (4 tablespoons) red wine
1 teaspoon thyme
cooking oil
salt and pepper

Vichy Carrots

Peel and slice carrots and place in a pan. Cover with stock and add all remaining ingredients except parsley. Bring to boil and simmer for 20 minutes. Turn up the heat and continue cooking until all the liquid has been used up and the carrots are coated with the glaze. Turn into a heated dish and sprinkle with parsley.

450 g (1 lb) carrots
25 g (1 oz) butter
1 tablespoon soft brown sugar
vegetable stock
salt and black pepper
finely chopped parsley

Pear and Ginger Crumble Pudding

Peel, core, and slice pears and chop ginger. Melt butter in a pan and add your favorite muesli mix and sugar. Place half the pears and ginger in an ovenproof dish and cover with half muesli mixture. Repeat these two layers and pour on the water and a little ginger syrup. Bake in a moderate oven 180°C/350°F for 1 hour. Serve hot or cold with fresh cream or yogurt.

700 g (1½ lb) pears
50 g (2 oz) butter
100 g (4 oz) muesli mix
50 g (2 oz) Barbados sugar
90 ml (6 tablespoons) water
1 piece of stem ginger and a little syrup

Country Vegetable Soup
Spinach Ravioli with Tomato Salad
Chocolate Mousse

Country Vegetable Soup

Melt butter in pan and gently fry chopped onion. Add remaining vegetables roughly chopped and continue to fry for a further 5 minutes. Add stock, Marmite, herbs, and seasoning. Bring to boil and simmer for 1 hour. Rub through a sieve or mouli. Correct seasoning and reheat.

450 g (1 lb) mixed vegetables: carrots, leeks, potatoes, celery, and turnips
2 onions
25 g (1 oz) butter
750 ml (1½ pints) vegetable stock
1 teaspoon Marmite or yeast extract
1 bay leaf
½ teaspoon marjoram
¼ teaspoon thyme
salt and pepper

Spinach Ravioli*

Put the flour and salt in a bowl. Make a hollow in the middle and add the oil and eggs. Mix well with a fork to form a dough. Roll out, fold in half, and replace in the bowl. Leave for 1 hour. Meanwhile finely chop onion and garlic and fry for 5 minutes in cooking oil. Add wine and simmer for 20 minutes. Season with salt, pepper, and nutmeg and add washed spinach. Cook for about 5 minutes. Remove from heat and add cheese, stirring well. Unfold pasta and roll out thinly. Cut into 4 cm (1½ in) squares and place a teaspoonful of the spinach mixture in the center of half the squares. Place a square of pasta on top of each, sealing the edge well with water. Bring water to boil and add salt. Cook the ravioli in the salted water for 10 minutes. Remove with a draining spoon and place on warmed plates. Pour over melted butter and sprinkle with Parmesan cheese. Serve immediately.

Pasta
350 g (12 oz) plain flour
4 eggs
15 ml (1 tablespoon) oil
salt

Filling
1 medium onion
1 clove garlic
225 g (8 oz) grated cheese
275 g (10 oz) spinach
125 ml (¼ pint) red wine
¼ teaspoon nutmeg
salt and pepper
cooking oil
2 liters (4 pints) salted
   water
50 g (2 oz) melted butter
50 g (2 oz) Parmesan
   cheese

Tomato Salad

Peel and slice tomatoes and slice cucumber. Place in a bowl with marjoram and seasoning. Add oil and vinegar well mixed and chill for ½ hour.

4 large Mediterranean
   tomatoes
10 cm (4 in) cucumber
1 teaspoon marjoram
60 ml (4 tablespoons)
   olive oil
30 ml (2 tablespoons)
   wine vinegar
salt and pepper

* See Plate 6.

Chocolate Mousse

Melt chocolate over hot water with a little water to achieve a creamy consistency. Separate the egg yolks from the whites and mix with chocolate. Whisk egg whites with a pinch of salt until really stiff. Add to chocolate mixture and pour into individual pots and place in refrigerator to set. Just before serving, sprinkle with flaked almonds.

100 g (4 oz) plain
  chocolate
3 eggs
a little water
flaked almonds
pinch of salt

menu

Shropska
Courgette and Oatmeal Savory
with Buttered Potatoes and Salad in Season
with Lemon Dressing
Orange Semolina Pudding
with Marmalade Sauce

Shropska

Coarsely chop all vegetables and layer in individual bowls. Top with salt and pepper, grated cheese, and lemon juice. Chill for 30–45 minutes.

4 large tomatoes
1 small onion
½ green pepper
10 cm (4 in) cucumber
3 sticks celery
100 g (4 oz) grated cheese
juice of 1 lemon
salt and pepper

Courgette (Zucchini) and Oatmeal Savory

Finely chop onions and fry in cooking oil until golden in color. Add oatmeal and continue cooking for 2–3 minutes. Add seasoning and stock, stirring all the time. Continue cooking for 10 minutes until mixture thickens. Meanwhile fry zucchini in oil until half cooked and peel and slice tomatoes. Place in an oven-proof dish. Beat eggs and add to oatmeal mixture. Stir in most of the cheese and pour over the vegetables. Top with remaining cheese. Bake at 190°C/375°F for about 45 minutes. Check the center is cooked through with a fork before serving.

2 large onions
450 g (1 lb) zucchini
4 tomatoes
cooking oil
4 tablespoons medium
  oatmeal
75 g (3 oz) cheese
4 eggs
250 ml (¼ pint) vegetable
  stock

Lemon Dressing

Place all ingredients in a bowl and beat well with a fork. Pour over the salad.

60 ml (4 tablespoons)
  salad oil
30 ml (2 tablespoons)
  lemon juice
1 teaspoon French
  mustard
½ teaspoon sugar
1 teaspoon finely
  chopped onion
1 teaspoon finely
  chopped parsley
black pepper

Orange Semolina Pudding with Marmalade Sauce

Place semolina in a pan with milk, butter, and honey and slowly bring to boil, stirring all the time. Simmer for 10–15 minutes and add grated orange rind. Serve in individual bowls.

To make sauce, place all ingredients in a pan and slowly heat through. Pour over the semolina and serve at once.

Pudding
50 g (2 oz) semolina
750 ml (1½ pints) milk
25 g (1 oz) butter
30 ml (2 tablespoons)
  milk
grated orange rind

Sauce
2 tablespoons orange
  marmalade
juice of 1 orange
15–30 ml (1–2
  tablespoons) water

menu

Mixed Pulse Soup with Herb Bread
Jerusalem Eggs, Braised Celery, and Steamed Carrots with Breton Tomato Salad
Baked Apples Seville

Mixed Pulse Soup

Soak peas and beans overnight. Drain and place in a pan with all the other ingredients except green vegetables and slowly bring to a boil. Simmer for 1–2 hours until all the vegetables are soft; 15 minutes before serving add green vegetables. Blend or sieve and serve with freshly chopped parsley sprinkled on top.

50 g (2 oz) dried red beans
25 g (1 oz) chick peas
25 g (1 oz) lentils
1·onion
750 ml (1½ pints) water
50 g (2 oz) green vegetables—spinach, cabbage, or lettuce
1 teaspoon chopped mint
¼ teaspoon ground cumin
pinch of tumeric
salt and pepper
freshly chopped parsley

Herb Bread

Soften butter and mix with herbs. Slice the French loaf into 8 slices. Butter each slice with the herb butter and press back into a loaf shape. Wrap in foil and bake at 230°C/450°F for about 5 minutes.

1 short French loaf
50 g (2 oz) butter
½ teaspoon mixed herbs
½ teaspoon thyme
½ teaspoon basil
½ teaspoon rosemary

Breton Tomato Salad

Wash and slice chicory and lay on a serving plate. Skin and slice tomatoes and place on top of the chicory. Sprinkle with black pepper. Mix yogurt, lemon juice, and sorrel and pour over the tomatoes. Garnish with a little more fresh sorrel around the edges. If fresh sorrel is not available, use 2 tablespoons young spinach leaves.

4–6 Mediterranean tomatoes
2 heads chicory
60 ml (4 tablespoons) yogurt
10 ml (2 teaspoons) lemon juice
½ teaspoon sugar
1 tablespoon finely chopped fresh sorrel or spinach
black pepper

Jerusalem Eggs

Peel and steam Jerusalem artichokes for about 10 minutes until cooked through. Boil potatoes and mash with 25 g (1 oz) butter, three-quarters of artichokes, and salt and pepper. Halve eggs and remove yolks and mash with remaining artichokes. Season and pile back into egg whites. Place in the base of a casserole dish. Melt remaining butter and make a roux sauce with the flour and milk and season to taste. Pour over the eggs. Spoon the potato and artichoke mixture around the edge of the dish and bake at 220°C/425°F for 20 minutes.

8 hard-boiled eggs
450 g (1 lb) Jerusalem
  artichokes
450 g (1 lb) potatoes
75 g (3 oz) butter
50 g (2 oz) flour
250 ml (½ pint) milk
salt and pepper

Braised Celery

Wash and trim celery heads. Cut in half and lay lengthways in a fireproof dish. Finely slice onion and lay on top of celery. Dissolve Marmite in hot water and pour over the vegetables. Season and bake in a moderate oven 180°C/350°F for 20 minutes, then raise temperature as for Jerusalem Eggs and continue cooking.

If the celery is to be cooked on its own, bake for 1 hour at original temperature.

2 celery heads
1 onion
1 teaspoon Marmite or
  yeast extract
100 ml (4 fl.oz) hot water
salt and pepper

Baked Apples Seville

Wash and core apples. Cut around the center to stop the apples splitting during cooking. Stuff with dates, ground almonds, and marmalade. Top with a little cider and bake at 220°C/425°F for ¾ hour.

4 cooking apples
12–16 dates
2 tablespoons Seville
  orange marmalade
4 teaspoons ground
  almonds, hazelnuts, or
  peanuts
cider

Chick Peas à la Greque
Stuffed Potatoes with Tomatoes
Coffee Ice Cream

Chick Peas à la Greque

Soak chick peas overnight and boil in water for about 1½ hours until almost cooked. Fry finely sliced onions in cooking oil until transparent. Add mushrooms, halved or quartered according to size. Drain chick peas and add to mushroom mixture. Pour over the wine and add all other ingredients. Bring to boil and simmer for 30 minutes. Serve chilled.

100 g (4 oz) chick peas
2 small onions
100 g (4 oz) mushrooms
2 teaspoons tomato paste
½ teaspoon oregano
1 bay leaf
500 ml (1 pint) white
  wine
salt and pepper
cooking oil

Stuffed Potatoes with Tomatoes

Scrub the potatoes and score the skins. Boil for 30 minutes in salted water. Drain and leave to cool. Slice the bottom off each potato so that it can stand unsupported. At the other end scoop out enough potato so that in the hollow there is enough room to hold an egg. Grease an ovenproof dish and place the potatoes on it. Wash the tomatoes and cut a cross on the top of each. Place them between the potatoes. Flake half the butter and dot over the vegetables. Lightly season and sprinkle with a little of the cheese. Break an egg into each potato. Now add the rest of the cheese and a little milk to each potato. Season again. Sprinkle with paprika and add the rest of the flaked butter. Bake at 220°C/450°F for 20 minutes.

8 large, round potatoes
4 tomatoes
50 g (2 oz) butter
salt and pepper
100 g (4 oz) grated
Emmental cheese
8 small eggs
30 ml (2 tablespoons)
milk
paprika
parsley

58

Coffee Ice Cream

Whip milk and cream until stiff. Whisk eggs and honey until thick and pale in color. Add instant coffee and whisk some more. Quickly fold into cream mixture and spoon into a container. Freeze at once.

3 eggs
1 tablespoon runny honey
125 ml (¼ pint) heavy cream
75 ml (3 fl.oz) milk
3–4 teaspoons instant coffee

---

menu

Leeks Vinaigrette
Barley Broth, French Bread, Spinach, and Watercress Salad
Grapefruit Ice Cream

Leeks Vinaigrette

Steam, wash, and coarsely chop leeks for about 8–10 minutes. Allow to cool. Finely slice onions and mix with leeks in individual bowls. Mix dressing and pour over leeks and onions. Sprinkle with finely chopped parsley.

6–8 medium leeks
1 small onion
fresh parsley

Dressing
90 ml (6 tablespoons) salad oil
30 ml (2 tablespoons) cider vinegar
¼ teaspoon French mustard
¼ teaspoon sugar
salt and pepper

Barley Broth

Finely chop onion and fry in cooking oil for about 5 minutes to soften. Add barley and lentils and pour on the stock. Sprinkle with herbs and seasoning and add baked beans. Bring to the boil and simmer for 1½–2 hours. Serve sprinkled with fresh parsley.

1 large onion
50 g (2 oz) flaked barley
25 g (1 oz) pearl barley
50 g (2 oz) lentils
1 small tin baked beans
1 liter (2 pints) vegetable stock
thyme and bay leaf
salt and pepper
cooking oil
fresh parsley

Spinach and Watercress Salad

Wash spinach and watercress. Shred and mix. Toss in dressing and herbs.

225 g (½ lb) small spinach leaves
½ bunch watercress
60 ml (4 tablespoons) oil and lemon dressing
½ teaspoon sweet basil and summer savory

Grapefruit Ice Cream

Whip all ingredients together until as stiff as possible. Spoon into a container. Cover and freeze.

250 ml (½ pint) heavy cream
150 ml (6 fl.oz) grapefruit juice
150 g (6 oz) sugar

Tomato Pasta Salad with Marinated Mushrooms
London Loaf with Buttered Green Beans
and New Potatoes
Coriander Apples

Tomato Pasta Salad

Cook pasta in boiling salted water. Just before the pasta is cooked, add frozen peas. Continue cooking for five minutes. Mix oil, vinegar, tomato paste, and seasoning. Drain pasta and peas and pour tomato dressing over the top. Leave to cool. Chop onion and celery finely and shred green pepper. Cube cheese. Mix all ingredients together and garnish with fried bread croûtons and chopped parsley.

100 g (4 oz) pasta
½ onion
3 sticks celery
¼ green pepper
50 g (2 oz) grated cheese
4 tablespoons frozen peas
2 tablespoons tomato paste
30 ml (2 tablespoons) salad oil
15 ml (1 tablespoon) vinegar
½ teaspoon oregano
salt and pepper
fried bread croûtons
chopped parsley

Marinated Mushrooms

Mix lemon juice, oil, tomato ketchup, thyme, and crushed clove of garlic. Finely slice mushrooms and pour over the marinade. Sprinkle with salt and black pepper. Leave to stand for 1–2 hours before serving.

450 g (1 lb) mushrooms
30 ml (2 tablespoons) lemon juice
60 ml (4 tablespoons) salad oil
15 ml (1 tablespoon) tomato ketchup
1 teaspoon thyme
1 clove garlic
salt and black pepper

61

London Loaf

Finely chop all vegetables and mix with dry ingredients, herbs, spices, and seasoning. Bind with beaten eggs and stock. Press into a baking pan approximately 30 × 20 cm (12 × 8 in). Bake at 200°C/400°F for 1 hour. If desired serve with tomato sauce.

75 g (3 oz) bread crumbs
150 g (6 oz) mixed nuts
  (peanuts, hazelnuts, and
  almonds)
2 onions
6 tomatoes
2 carrots
100 g (4 oz) mushrooms
4 sticks celery
150 ml (6 fl.oz) vegetable
  stock
2 eggs
25 g (1 oz) ground
  sesame seeds (optional)
1½ teaspoons ground
  cumin
½ teaspoon celery seed
  or celery salt
4 tablespoons freshly
  chopped parsley
salt and pepper

Coriander Apples

Dissolve honey and sugar in cider. Peel, core, and slice apples and lay in a fireproof dish. Sprinkle with coriander and pour over the sweetened cider. Cover and bake for 30–40 minutes at 200°C/400°F. Serve with fresh cream or custard.

4 Bramley cooking apples
200 ml (8 fl.oz) cider
2 teaspoons honey
2 teaspoons Barbados
  sugar
½ teaspoon coriander

Cold Meals and Salads 6

This chapter includes 12 full menus and a selection of 12 individual salad recipes.

menu

**Asparagus with Fresh Mint
and Sour Cream Sauce
Sliced Peanut Loaf with Beanshoot and Onion
Salad,* and Green Potato Salad and Tomatoes
Peaches in White Wine**

Asparagus with Fresh Mint and Sour Cream Sauce

Steam asparagus, drain, and allow to cool. Mix sour cream with mint and seasoning. Arrange asparagus on individual plates and cover the tips with sauce.

1 lb asparagus (fresh or
 frozen)
1 small carton sour cream
1 tablespoon freshly
 chopped mint
salt and pepper

*See page 79.

63

Sliced Peanut Loaf

Finely chop onions, mushrooms, and tomatoes and add all other ingredients except oatmeal. Mix well and roll in oatmeal. Shape into a loaf and place on a greased tray. Bake at 180°C/350°F for 45 minutes–1 hour. Allow to cool and serve sliced.

100 g (4 oz) mushrooms
3 onions
2 tomatoes
2 tablespoons peanut
  butter
50 g (2 oz) ground
  peanuts
50 g (2 oz) soya flour
50 g (2 oz) bread crumbs
2 eggs
2 teaspoons dill weed
salt and pepper
25 g (1 oz) oatmeal

Green Potato Salad

Cook potatoes and dice hot. Mix dressing and pour over warm potatoes. Leave to cool and add chopped green salad items just before serving.

350 g (12 oz) potatoes
1 head chicory
1 small bunch chives
watercress
4–6 Cos lettuce leaves

Dressing
90 ml (6 tablespoons) oil
45 ml (3 tablespoons)
  wine vinegar
1 teaspoon French
  mustard
a little sugar
salt and black pepper

Peaches in White Wine

Place wine, sugar, lemon juice, and spices in a pan and bring to boil. Continue boiling for 5 minutes. Turn down the heat and add whole peaches. Simmer for about 5–8 minutes, turning from time to time. Remove from heat as soon as peaches soften. Leave to stand in the refrigerator for at least 2 hours, turning from time to time.

4 peaches
250 ml (½ pint) white
  wine
1 tablespoon honey
5 ml (1 teaspoon) lemon
  juice
¼ teaspoon mixed spices

Melon and Cucumber Salad
"Scotch" Eggs with Raw Fennel Salad
and American Coleslaw*
Apricot Meringue Gâteau

Melon and Cucumber Salad

Dice the melon and cucumber. Finely chop the mint and mix with yogurt and mayonnaise. Season to taste. Put in individual bowls and garnish with 2 or 3 mint leaves.

½ honeydew melon
7.5 cm (3 in) cucumber
3 sprigs mint
15 ml (1 tablespoon) yogurt
15 ml (1 tablespoon) mayonnaise
salt and pepper

"Scotch" Eggs**

Hard-boil eggs and leave to cool. Make a panada with flour, butter, and milk. Add buckwheat and continue cooking for 5 minutes. Add peanuts and seasoning and leave to cool. Divide peanut mixture into 4 and shape around each egg. Dip in beaten egg and bread crumbs and deep fry.

4 large eggs
50 g (2 oz) buckwheat flour
100 g (4 oz) ground peanuts
50 g (2 oz) plain flour
50 g (2 oz) butter
300 ml (12 fl.oz) milk
salt and pepper
50 g (2 oz) dried bread crumbs
1 beaten egg

*See page 83.
**See Plate 2 (bottom).

65

Raw Fennel Salad

Chop all ingredients finely and mix with herbs and pepper. Toss in dressing and serve at once.

1 medium fennel heart
8 radishes
4 spring onions
2 sticks celery
30 ml (2 tablespoons) oil and vinegar dressing
½ teaspoon marjoram
black pepper

Apricot Meringue Gâteau

Soak apricots in water overnight. Whisk egg whites very stiffly and then gradually whisk in half the sugar. Fold in the rest of the sugar with the nuts, bicarbonate of soda, and vanilla essence. Spread the meringue into 2 thin equal-sized rounds on rice paper on a baking sheet. Bake in a low oven 130°C/250°F for about 2½ hours until dried out. Allow to cool on a wire rack. Drain apricots and simmer with honey and 125 ml (¼ pint) water for 30 minutes until soft. Purée and allow to cool. Whisk cream until thick. Place a layer of meringue on a serving dish and spread with apricot purée and then with cream. Top with the second layer of meringue and sprinkle with chopped nuts.

Meringue
2 egg whites
100 g (4 oz) caster sugar
50 g (2 oz) ground hazelnuts
pinch bicarbonate of soda
vanilla essence

Filling
100 g (4 oz) dried apricots
125 ml (¼ pint) water
1 tablespoon honey
125 ml (¼ pint) heavy cream

menu

Avocado with Orange
Egg and Almond Salad with Cumin Cabbage
Chocolate Truffle Pudding

Avocado with Orange

Peel oranges and remove pith and center core. Chop and mix with mayonnaise. Add marjoram, coriander, and seasoning to taste. Halve and stone avocados and fill the centers with orange sauce. Serve remaining sauce in a bowl.

2 avocados
2 oranges
30 ml (2 tablespoons) mayonnaise
sprinkle of coriander
½ teaspoon marjoram
salt and pepper

Egg and Almond Salad

Dice all ingredients except tomato and parsley and mix with the seasoning and mayonnaise. Heap onto a serving dish and surround with sliced tomato. Sprinkle with parsley.

6 hard-boiled eggs
2 tablespoons flaked almonds
150 g (2 oz) Cheshire cheese
4 beetroot
½ cucumber
4 spring onions
50 g (2 oz) mushrooms
4 tomatoes
chopped parsley
60 ml (4 tablespoons) mayonnaise
salt and pepper

Cumin Cabbage

Mix cumin seed with oil and lemon dressing. Season to taste and pour over shredded cabbage and watercress.

½ medium hearted cabbage
½ bunch watercress
60 ml (4 tablespoons) oil and lemon dressing
¼ teaspoon ground cumin seed
salt and pepper

Chocolate Truffle Pudding

Melt butter and honey or sugar in a pan. Do not allow to boil. Remove from heat and add cocoa, crumbs, nuts, and raisins. Stir well and add chosen liquor. Press into a small pan about 10 cm (4 in) square and decorate with walnut halves. Place in refrigerator to set. Serve in small squares with freshly whipped cream.

150 g (6 oz) stale cake crumbs
50 g (2 oz) butter
50 g (2 oz) thick honey or Barbados sugar
1 tablespoon cocoa
1 tablespoon chopped walnuts
1 tablespoon raisins
15 ml (1 tablespoon) sherry, rum, or brandy
4 walnut halves

menu

Iced Cucumber Soup
Orange Banana Salad with Senegal Eggs*
and Watercress, and Bean and Garlic Salad
Coffee Cheesecake Mousse

Iced Cucumber Soup**

Melt butter in pan and fry chopped onions till golden. Add wine and bring to boil. Add sliced potatoes, cucumber, vegetable stock, and seasoning. Simmer for 30 minutes and allow to cool. Blend and correct seasoning. Serve chilled, garnished with fresh cream, chopped parsley, and diced cucumber.

225 g (8 oz) potatoes
½ large cucumber
1 medium onion
50 g (1 oz) butter
125 ml (¼ pint) white wine
500 ml (1 pint) vegetable stock
salt and pepper
chopped parsley
2.5 cm (1 in) diced cucumber
60 ml (4 tablespoons) reg. cream

*See page 166; divide quantities by three.
**See Plate 3.

Orange Banana Salad

Mix the peanut butter, orange peel, and ginger if used. Spread this mixture onto one-half of each banana, then top with remaining halves. Cut each into four. Mix mayonnaise with orange juice. Dip filled banana pieces into this and roll in chopped peanuts till coated. Serve on lettuce leaves.

2 tablespoons smooth peanut butter
1 teaspoon finely grated orange peel
25 g (1 oz) finely chopped crystallized ginger (optional)
2 bananas, split lengthwise
30 ml (2 tablespoons) mayonnaise
7 ml (½ tablespoon) orange juice
50 g (2 oz) chopped peanuts, fresh or roasted
lettuce leaves

Bean and Garlic Salad

Cook beans (see Chapter 4). Finely chop onion, celery, pickled cucumber, garlic, and parsley. Mix with beans. Mix dressing with Worcestershire sauce. Pour over the bean mixture and season to taste. Serve garnished with watercress.

100 g (4 oz) haricot beans
½ onion
1 stick celery
1 large pickled gherkin/cucumber
3 tablespoons parsley
30 ml (2 tablespoons) oil and vinegar dressing
7 ml (½ teaspoon) Worcestershire sauce
1 clove garlic
watercress
salt and pepper

Coffee Cheesecake Mousse

Base

Crush digestive biscuits* and mix with sugar and melted butter. Press into a 17.5 cm (7 in) cake pan and place in a low oven 140°C/275°F for 8–10 minutes. Allow to cool. Mix honey and cream cheese until smooth and gradually add egg yolks and yogurt. Boil water and mix with coffee and gelatine or gelozone. Allow to cool and mix with cream cheese and eggs. Whisk egg whites until stiff and fold into the cream cheese mixture. Pour on top of base and chill until firm.

Base
9 digestive biscuits
40 g (1½ oz) butter
25 g (1 oz) sugar

Filling
225 g (8 oz) cream cheese
2 tablespoons honey
125 ml (¼ pint) natural
  yogurt
1 tablespoon instant
  coffee
65 ml (2½ fl.oz) water
12½ g (½ oz) gelatine or
  2 teaspoons gelozone
2 eggs

menu

French Tomato Salad
Stuffed Eggs with Mixed Bean Salad,
Carrot and Orange Salad and Potato Salad**
Black Currant Ice Cream

French Tomato Salad

Peel and slice tomatoes and arrange on four plates. Finely slice onion and lay on top of the tomatoes. Sprinkle with chervil. Mix all remaining ingredients to make a dressing and pour over the salad. Serve slightly chilled.

4 large Mediterranean
  tomatoes
1 onion
chervil
90 ml (6 tablespoons)
  olive oil
45 ml (3 tablespoons)
  wine vinegar
½ teaspoon French
  mustard
½ teaspoon sugar
salt and pepper

*These (British) thin and slightly sweet wafers may be purchased in some supermarkets and specialty stores. However, other crackers generally used for pie crust may be substituted.
**See page 81.

Stuffed Eggs

Halve eggs and remove yolks. Mix with the chosen stuffing ingredients and pile back into the egg whites. Sprinkle with paprika or chopped parsley to garnish.

4 hard-boiled eggs

Stuffing 1
10 ml (2 teaspoons) mayonnaise
2 teaspoons chutney
salt and pepper

or

Stuffing 2
20 ml (4 teaspoons) mayonnaise
½ teaspoon cumin or curry powder
salt and pepper

or

Stuffing 3
15 ml (3 teaspoons) mayonnaise
4 teaspoons grated blue cheese
salt and pepper

or

Stuffing 4
20 ml (4 teaspoons) mayonnaise
1 teaspoon ground walnuts
1 teaspoon marjoram

Mixed Bean Salad

Cook beans as directed in Chapter 4. Finely chop spring onions and mix with beans. Pour over the dressing and season to taste.

25 g (1 oz) haricot beans
25 g (1 oz) blackeye
    beans
25 g (1 oz) soya beans
25 g (1 oz) red beans
4 spring onions
60 ml (4 tablespoons) oil
    and vinegar dressing
black pepper

Carrot and Orange Salad

Peel and coarsely grate carrots. Peel and chop one orange and squeeze the other. Add chopped orange and juice to the carrot and mix well. Use plenty of black pepper to season. Decorate with olives.

2 large carrots
2 oranges
4 black olives
black pepper

Black Currant Ice Cream

Make the purée by simmering fruit in a little water and blending. Mix in the sugar or honey. Whip cream until stiff and fold into the fruit mixture. Spoon into a container, cover, and freeze.

250 ml (½ pint) heavy
    cream
250 ml (½ pint) black
    currant purée
2 tablespoons Barbados
    sugar or honey

menu

African Fruit Salad
Napoleon Rice Cake with Indian Onion Salad
and Cabbage and Pineapple Salad
Aduki Pie

African Fruit Salad

Place one large lettuce leaf on each dish and fill with peeled and chopped orange and grapefruit. Sprinkle with peanuts and chopped mint and add a tablespoon of dressing to each dish.

4 large Cos lettuce leaves
2 oranges
2 grapefruit
50 g (2 oz) roast peanuts
60 ml (4 tablespoons) oil
  and vinegar dressing
mint

Napoleon Rice Cake

Cook rice and peas, separately, in boiling salted water until tender. Drain and allow to cool. Chop nuts and onion and mix with rice and peas. Add herbs, dressing, and seasoning. Press into a greased pudding basin and chill for 1 hour. Carefully turn out onto serving dish and reshape if necessary. Garnish with sliced beetroot just before serving.

150 g (6 oz) rice
150 g (6 oz) fresh or
  frozen peas
75 g (3 oz) walnuts
75 g (3 oz) almonds
1 onion
1 teaspoon thyme
salt and pepper
15 ml (1 tablespoon) oil
  and vinegar dressing
2 cooked beetroot

Indian Onion Salad

Slice onions finely and fry in a mixture of butter and cooking oil with curry powder. When soft, drain off excess oil and add remaining ingredients. Continue cooking for 5 minutes, stirring all the time. Allow to cool ard serve chilled.

450 g (1 lb) large onions
25 g (1 oz) raisins
1 tablespoon Barbados
  sugar
30 ml (2 tablespoons)
  vinegar
1 teaspoon curry powder
butter and cooking oil

Cabbage and Pineapple Salad

Finely shred cabbage. Drain pineapple and mix with cabbage. Add lemon juice and sage and mix well.

1 small or ½ large green hearted cabbage
1 small can crushed pineapple
juice of 1 lemon
1 sprig fresh or ¼ teaspoon dried sage

Aduki Pie

Rub fat into flour and salt and bind with water. Roll out thinly and line a 17.5 cm (7 in) flan pan. Place beans and raisins in base of flan. Cover with peeled, sliced apples. Pour over lemon and honey and sprinkle with cinnamon. Brush with apricot jam. Bake at 200°C/400°F for 45–50 minutes.

Pastry
100 g (4 oz) plain flour
50 g (2 oz) margarine or butter
pinch salt
water

Filling
75 g (3 oz) cooked Aduki beans
50 g (2 oz) raisins
450 g (1 lb) cooking apples
juice of 1 lemon
2 tablespoons honey
cinnamon
apricot jam

menu

Courgettes Vinaigrette
Tomato and Oregano Cheesecake
with Savory Rice* and Waldorf Salad
Fresh Orange Compôte

*See page 82.

Courgettes (Zucchini) Vinaigrette

Wash zucchini and slice large ones in half lengthways. Cut into 2.5 cm (1 in) lengths and steam in a very little salted water for about 5–8 minutes until just tender. Drain and allow to cool. Finely slice onion and arrange with zucchini in small individual bowls. Mix oil, vinegar, French mustard, and sugar and pour over the zucchini. Sprinkle with black pepper and parsley. Chill for 30 minutes before serving.

4 large or 8 small
  zucchini
1 large onion
90 ml (6 tablespoons) oil
45 ml (3 tablespoons)
  wine vinegar
½ teaspoon sugar
1 tablespoon chopped
  parsley
½ teaspoon French
  mustard
salt and black pepper

Tomato and Oregano Cheesecake

Crush biscuits and mix with melted butter. Press into 17.5 cm (7 in) cake pan and bake at 140°C/275°F for 8 minutes. Remove and allow to cool. Place cottage cheese and contents of a can of tomatoes in a blender and blend. Prepare gelatine or gelozone as suggested in Chapter 4 and add to cheese and tomato mixture. Add oregano and seasoning and pour over the cold biscuit base. Refrigerate until set. Remove from cake pan and serve.

Base
10 unsweetened
  wheatmeal biscuits
40 g (1½ oz) butter

Filling
225 g (8 oz) cottage
  cheese
1 can tomatoes
12½ g (½ oz) package
  gelatine or 2 teaspoons
  gelozone
1 teaspoon oregano
water
salt and pepper

Waldorf Salad

Dice apples, celery, and walnuts. Mix together with mayonnaise and black pepper.

2 eating apples
4 sticks celery
8 half walnuts
15 ml (1 tablespoon)
  mayonnaise
black pepper

Fresh Orange Compôte

Peel and slice four of the oranges and arrange in a bowl. Grate a little of the rind of the remaining oranges over the slices. Squeeze the juice and pour over the rest of the fruit. Pour over the Cointreau and chill. For those with a very sweet tooth, add 1 tablespoon of honey to the orange juice before pouring over the fruit.

5 oranges
1 miniature bottle
  Cointreau
1 tablespoon honey
  (optional)

menu

Mushrooms in Red Wine
Pasta Nut Salad with Asparagus and Soya Bean
Salad and Endive with Rosemary
Assorted Fresh Fruit Bowl

Mushrooms in Red Wine

Finely slice onions and fry in cooking oil until transparent. Add mushrooms and sauté for a further 2–3 minutes. Add all remaining ingredients and bring to boil. Simmer for 30 minutes and allow to cool. Chill before serving sprinkled with freshly chopped parsley.

225 g (8 oz) button
  mushrooms
2 onions
300 ml (12 fl.oz) red wine
¼ teaspoon thyme
¼ teaspoon garlic salt
½ teaspoon fennel seed
2 teaspoons tomato purée
salt and pepper
parsley

Pasta Nut Salad

Cook pasta in boiling salted water until tender. Drain and allow to cool. Finely chop onions and green pepper and mix with pasta. Add nuts and raisins, yogurt, and lemon juice and mix well. Garnish with a few more flaked almonds and raisins.

100 g (4 oz) pasta shells
50 g (2 oz) roasted
   peanuts
50 g (2 oz) flaked
   almonds
50 g (2 oz) raisins
1 green pepper
1 shallott or 3 spring
   onions
1 small carton natural
   yogurt
15 ml (1 tablespoon)
   lemon juice

Asparagus and Soya Bean Salad

Drain asparagus and chop. Mix with soya beans and add very finely chopped celery and gherkin. Sprinkle with basil and black pepper and toss in oil and vinegar dressing.

150 g (6 oz) cooked soya
   beans
75 g (3 oz) can of
   asparagus
2 sticks of celery
1 teaspoon basil
2 gherkins
black pepper
30 ml (2 tablespoons) oil
   and vinegar dressing

Endive with Rosemary

Wash curly endive and tear into pieces. Mix rosemary with dressing and toss the endive in the mixture. Sprinkle with black pepper.

½ large head curly
   endive
2 teaspoons ground
   rosemary
45 ml (3 tablespoons) oil
   and vinegar dressing
black pepper

Iced Beetroot Soup
Peanut and Garlic Pâté with French Bread and
Beanshoot and Onion Salad
Pears in Orange Juice with Baked Egg Custard

Iced Beetroot Soup

Heat stock and dissolve Marmite in it. Allow to cool. Blend beetroot, stock, and yogurt in a blender. Add cream and season. Serve chilled with a little fresh orange juice poured in just before serving. Add ice cubes and mint.

450 g (1 lb) cooked beetroot
125 ml (¼ pint) vegetable stock
½ teaspoon Marmite or yeast extract
1 small carton yogurt
½ small carton heavy cream
juice of 1 orange
salt and pepper
2 sprigs mint
6 ice cubes

Peanut and Garlic Pâté

Mix all ingredients together until smooth and season to taste. Serve chilled in individual dishes with crusty French bread.

3 tablespoons peanut butter
100 g (4 oz) cream cheese
2 finely chopped cloves garlic
30 ml (2 tablespoons) reg. cream
few drops Worcestershire or Tabasco sauce
salt and pepper

Beanshoot and Onion Salad

Wash spring onions and slice lengthways. Finely slice green pepper and mix with onions and beanshoots. Toss in dressing and sprinkle with black pepper.

350 g (12 oz) beanshoots
1 bunch spring onions
½ green pepper
45 ml (3 tablespoons) oil and vinegar dressing
black pepper

Pears in Orange Juice

Squeeze oranges and mix honey with the juice. Peel, halve, and core the pears and pour over the orange juice. Chill and just before serving sprinkle with chopped nuts.

2 large ripe pears
2 oranges
1 tablespoon chopped nuts
1 teaspoon honey (optional)

Baked Egg Custard

Beat eggs with honey and add warmed milk. Pour into a greased pie plate. Stand the pie plate in a tray of warm water and bake slowly at 170°C/325°F until the custard is set in the center. This will take about 1 hour. Leave to cool.

500 ml (1 pint) milk
2 eggs
25 g (1 oz) honey
nutmeg

menu

Artichokes with Renaissance Sauce
Rocky Mountain Salad
with Orange and Watercress Salad
Stuffed Apricots

Artichokes with Renaissance Sauce

Boil the artichokes in salted water with a little lemon juice for 45 minutes. The leaves should come away easily when the artichokes are cooked. Remove center leaves and choke and allow to cool. Mix all ingredients of sauce together and spoon into the center of each artichoke. Sprinkle with paprika pepper just before serving.

4 artichokes
lemon juice
salt

Sauce
250 ml (½ pint) natural
   yogurt
1 tablespoon tomato
   paste
1 small chopped onion
1 teaspoon dill seed
salt and pepper
paprika pepper

Rocky Mountain Salad*

Cook rice in boiling salted water. Drain and leave to cool. Hard boil eggs and chop finely. Mix rice and eggs and add finely chopped gherkins and green pepper. Mix with mayonnaise, rosemary, and seasoning and pack into a greased pudding dish. Chill for 1 hour. Mix beans together and add finely chopped onion and parsley and toss in dressing. Turn out the rice mixture onto a serving dish and surround with bean salad.

Center
150 g (6 oz) rice
3 eggs
1 small green pepper
3 large gherkins
15 ml (1 tablespoon)
   mayonnaise
1 teaspoon rosemary
salt and pepper

Surround
225 g (8 oz) cooked red
   kidney beans
100 g (4 oz) cooked broad
   beans
50 g (2 oz) cooked haricot
   or blackeye beans
1 small onion
1 tablespoon chopped
   parsley
60 ml (4 tablespoons) oil
   and vinegar dressing

*See Plate 2 (top).

Orange and Watercress Salad

Wash and chop watercress. Peel and slice oranges retaining any juice that runs out. Mix watercress and sprinkle with black pepper and olives.

1 bunch watercress
2 oranges
8 black olives
black pepper

Stuffed Apricots

Simmer apricots in wine and honey for about 15–20 minutes until soft. Allow to cool. Mix cream, sugar, wine, and brandy and whisk until fairly thick. Halve and stone apricots and place on a flat dish. Fill each half with brandy cream and add the juice to the base of the fruit.

8 apricots
125 ml (¼ pint) white wine
1 teaspoon honey

Filling
125 ml (¼ pint) heavy cream
40 g (1½ oz) Barbados sugar
50 ml (2 fl.oz) white wine
25 ml (1 fl.oz) brandy

menu

Salad Medley

Potato Salad

Peel and boil potatoes in salted water until soft. Drain and chop. Add finely chopped onion and parsley and mix with mayonnaise and dressing while still hot. Leave to cool and season before serving.

450 g (1 lb) potatoes
1 small onion
parsley
15 ml (1 tablespoon) mayonnaise
30 ml (2 tablespoons) oil and vinegar dressing
salt and pepper

Red Cabbage and Walnut Salad

Very finely chop or grate cabbage and finely chop celery and walnuts. Mix with mayonnaise and season.

½ small red cabbage
2 sticks celery
25 g (1 oz) walnuts
15 ml (1 tablespoon) mayonnaise
salt and pepper

Savory Rice

Boil rice in salted water until just cooked. Wash in cold water and drain well. Finely chop mushrooms and green pepper and add to the rice with the sweet corn. Mix oil, vinegar, thyme, celery seed, or salt and black pepper and mix into the rice salad.

75 g (3 oz) rice
100 g (4 oz) mushrooms
225 g (8 oz) can sweet corn
½ green pepper
15 ml (1 tablespoon) oil
15 ml (1 tablespoon) vinegar
½ teaspoon thyme
½ teaspoon celery seed or salt
black pepper

Winter Salad

Grate carrots and cheese and mix with finely chopped sprouts. Add oil, cumin seed, lemon juice, and a little lemon rind and mix well. Pile into the center of a serving dish and garnish with red vegetables around the outside.

100 g (4 oz) Cheddar cheese
2 large carrots
225 g (8 oz) sprouts
1 lemon
5 ml (1 teaspoon) olive oil
½ teaspoon cumin seed
beetroot, tomato, or red pepper to garnish

Cheese
and Beanshoot Salad

Dice mushrooms, green pepper, and cheese. Mix with beanshoots, herbs, and seasoning. Toss in dressing and serve at once.

100 g (4 oz) beanshoots
100 g (4 oz) mushrooms
1 green pepper
100 g (4 oz) Caerphilly
  cheese
60 ml (4 tablespoons) oil
  and vinegar dressing
salt and pepper
sweet basil

Sprout
and Celery Salad

Finely chop sprouts, celery, and mushrooms and mix with nuts and raisins. Add marjoram, seasoning, and dressing.

150 g (6 oz) sprouts
½ head celery
100 g (4 oz) mushrooms
3 tablespoons raisins
3 tablespoons cashew
  nuts
marjoram
60 ml (4 tablespoons) oil
  and vinegar dressing
salt and pepper

American Coleslaw

Shred cabbage as finely as possible and add all other ingredients. Mix well and season. Add a little mustard if liked.

½ small white cabbage
1 small grated carrot
¼ small finely sliced
  green pepper
1 grated apple
1 tablespoon flaked
  almonds
1 tablespoon raisins
45 ml (3 tablespoons)
  mayonnaise
salt and pepper

Carrot, Raisin and Peanut Salad

Grate carrots and immediately mix with oil. Add all other ingredients and serve at once.

2 large carrots
1 tablespoon raisins
2 tablespoons roast
  peanuts
30 ml (2 tablespoons) oil
15 ml (1 tablespoon)
  lemon juice
black pepper
½ teaspoon dill weed

Beetroot Cream Salad

Cook beetroot and allow to cool. Dice and mix with diced gherkin and sour cream. Add basil and black pepper.

450 g (1 lb) beetroot
1 carton sour cream
1 large gherkin
¼ teaspoon basil
black pepper

Cucumber and Olive Salad

Coarsely dice cucumber and mix with finely chopped pepper and olives. Mix oregano and black pepper in the dressing and pour over the salad.

½ cucumber
8–12 black olives
¼ red pepper or pimento
30 ml (2 tablespoons) oil
  and vinegar dressing
½ teaspoon oregano
black pepper

Red and Green Pepper Salad

Finely slice pepper. Mix cream cheese and mayonnaise and season. Pour over the pepper and serve garnished with parsley.

1 green pepper
1 red pepper
50 g (2 oz) cream cheese
15 ml (1 tablespoon)
  mayonnaise
salt and pepper
parsley

Quick Meals and Snacks 7

This chapter includes 12 menus plus 12 quick snack recipes.

Melon and Mushroom Salad
Butter Bean Country Casserole
with Spring Greens
Orange Syllabub

Melon and Mushroom Salad

Dice melon, mushrooms, and celery and mix with mayonnaise, herbs, and seasoning. Serve on a bed of chopped watercress.

½ melon
100 g (4 oz) button
    mushrooms
2 sticks celery
½ bunch watercress
30 ml (2 tablespoons)
    mayonnaise
salt and pepper
¼ teaspoon marjoram

85

Butter Bean Country Casserole

Finely slice onions and sauté until transparent. Add sliced mushrooms and continue frying for 5–6 minutes. Drain beans and chop tomatoes and add to the onions and mushrooms. Season and heat through. Place in ovenproof dish and sprinkle with grated cheese and bread crumbs. Brown under the grill and serve at once.

2 × 425 g (15 oz) cans butter beans
350 g (12 oz) mushrooms
4 small onions
6–8 tomatoes
100 g (4 oz) bread crumbs
100 g (4 oz) cheese
cooking oil
salt and pepper

Orange Syllabub

Grate orange rind into a measuring cup and then add juice. Make up to 150 ml (6 fl.oz) with liqueur. Leave to stand for 1 hour or so. Then add sugar and cream, whip to a thick creamy consistency. Serve with *petit fours* or ladyfingers.

1 orange
75 g (3 oz) Barbados sugar
250 ml (½ pint) heavy cream
Orange Curaçao or Cointreau

menu

Peach and Chicory Salad
Chili Bean Pie with Swiss Chard or Spinach
Fruit and Nut Case

Peach
and Chicory Salad

Drain peaches and chop into cubes. Finely chop pepper and slice chicory. Mix with peaches. Add almonds and sweet basil. Mix oil and vinegar and add to the peach and chicory mixture with black pepper to taste. Mix well and serve slightly chilled.

1 small can sliced peaches
3 heads of chicory
1 tablespoon flaked
  almonds
½ red pepper
1 teaspoon sweet basil
30 ml (2 tablespoons) oil
15 ml (1 tablespoon)
  vinegar
black pepper

Chili Bean Pie

Slice zucchini and fry gently in cooking oil with oregano, black pepper, and garlic salt. Cook peas in salted boiling water. Cook potatoes, drain, and mash with butter and milk and black pepper. Drain zucchini and peas and mix with can of beans. Heat through and spoon into an earthenware dish. Top with mashed potato. Fork and grill for 5 minutes until brown.

4 zucchini
100 g (4 oz) frozen peas
425 g (15 oz) can red
  beans in chili sauce
3 large potatoes
butter
milk
1 teaspoon oregano
½ teaspoon garlic salt
black pepper
cooking oil

Fruit and Nut Case

Arrange dried fruit and nuts in an attractive pattern on a large serving dish. Break chocolate into pieces and scatter among the fruit.

4 dried bananas
8 dates
4 dried prunes
8 dried apricots
1 tablespoon hazelnuts
1 tablespoon cashew nuts
1 tablespoon walnuts
100 g (4 oz) plain
  chocolate

Blue Cheese Dip with Toasted Rolls
Eggs Florentine
Orange Delight

Blue Cheese Dip with Toasted Rolls

Finely grate cheese and onion and mix with sour cream. Season with black pepper. Place in a blender for a few seconds. Halve rolls and toast under a really hot grill. Serve at once.

4 whole meal rolls (see page 49)
125 ml (¼ pint) sour cream
125 g (5 oz) blue cheese
75 g (3 oz) Cheddar cheese
½ small onion
black pepper

Eggs Florentine

Cook spinach and drain thoroughly. Make a roux sauce with the butter, flour, and milk, and season. Place spinach in a casserole dish and make four depressions in it. Break the eggs into these holes and cover with sauce. Sprinkle with nutmeg and bread crumbs and bake for 10 minutes at 200°C/400°F.

450 g (1 lb) fresh or frozen spinach
4 eggs
25 g (1 oz) butter
25 g (1 oz) flour
250 ml (½ pint) milk
25 g (1 oz) bread crumbs
nutmeg
salt and pepper

Orange Delight

Grate the rind of two oranges and mix with wheat germ and then peel and segment them. Dip segments in yogurt and then roll in either wheat germ and orange rind or in coconut. Arrange on a plate and serve with a few maraschino cherries for decoration.

4 oranges
2 tablespoons wheat germ
2 tablespoons dessicated coconut
yogurt
Maraschino cherries

Piquant Onions
Pasta with Peanut Sauce and Garlic Bread
Brie and Celery

Piquant Onions

Peel and slice onions and fry in butter. Add all other
ingredients and continue to cook for 15 minutes or
until the onions are soft. Serve in individual dishes
sprinkled with freshly chopped parsley.

450 g (1 lb) onions
25 g (1 oz) butter
1 teaspoon tomato paste
¼ teaspoon chili powder
5 ml (1 teaspoon)
  Worcestershire sauce
10 ml (2 teaspoons)
  vinegar
5 ml (1 teaspoon) soya
  sauce
salt and pepper
parsley

Pasta
with Peanut Sauce

Cook pasta in boiling salted water. Finely grate onion
and carrot and sauté in butter. Add peanut butter and
stir in the milk and lemon juice. Add sufficient water
to give a smooth creamy consistency. Bring to boil and
simmer for 5 minutes, adding more water if necessary.
Drain pasta and toss in butter. Serve with peanut sauce
poured over the top.

450 g (1 lb) pasta

Sauce
1 small onion
1 carrot
2 tablespoons peanut
  butter
30 ml (2 tablespoons)
  lemon juice
125 ml (¼ pint) milk
water
butter

Garlic Bread

Finely chop garlic and mix with butter. Slice French bread, but do not cut completely through the base. Butter each slice and wrap in foil. Place in a very hot oven 250°C/500°F for 5 minutes.

1 small French bread
2–3 cloves garlic
75 g (3 oz) butter

---

menu

Breton Mushrooms
Cauliflower Macaroni with Green Salad
Honey and Ginger Yogurt

Breton Mushrooms

Finely chop garlic and fry in butter. Add finely sliced mushrooms. Sprinkle with thyme and seasoning. Fry mushrooms gently for about 5–8 minutes until soft. Serve at once.

350 g (12 oz) mushrooms
50 g (2 oz) butter
2 cloves garlic
1 teaspoon thyme
salt and pepper

Cauliflower Macaroni

Cook macaroni and cauliflower, separately, in salted water. Make a roux sauce with the butter, flour, and milk. Add most of the cheese and season. Place macaroni and cauliflower, broken into pieces, in a casserole dish and cover with sauce. Lay slices of tomato on top and sprinkle with remaining cheese and bread crumbs. Place under the grill to brown.

225 g (8 oz) macaroni
100 g (4 oz) cheese
50 g (2 oz) bread crumbs
2 tomatoes
500 ml (1 pint) milk
25 g (1 oz) butter
25 g (1 oz) flour
salt and pepper

Honey and Ginger Yogurt

Chop stem ginger. Mix yogurt with honey and ginger syrup. Add ground and stem ginger and chill while the rest of the meal is being prepared.

500 ml (1 pint) plain yogurt
2 tablespoons runny honey
¼ teaspoon ground ginger
4 pieces stem ginger plus a little syrup

menu

Dutch Beet Salad
Soufflé Omelette with Domodoa Sauce,
New Potatoes, and Spinach Mountain
Banana Nut Dessert

Dutch Beet Salad

Dice beetroot, cheese, cucumber, and gherkin and toss in mayonnaise. Add coriander and seasoning. Serve on a bed of curly endive.

4 cooked beetroot
50 g (2 oz) Edam cheese
7.5 cm (3 in) cucumber
1 large gherkin
15 ml (1 tablespoon) mayonnaise
¼ teaspoon coriander
salt and pepper
curly endive

Soufflé Omelette

Separate yolks from whites and mix yolks with milk and seasoning. Whip egg whites until really stiff and fold in the yolk mixture. Pour into a frying pan with hot fat ready and cook for about 3–4 minutes until the base is set. Finish off for another 3–4 minutes under the grill. Serve at once.

6 eggs
a little milk
salt and pepper

Domodoa Sauce

Heat oil in a pan and fry onion in it with the turmeric until transparent. Add all remaining ingredients and bring to boil. Simmer for 10 minutes.

30 ml (2 tablespoons)
   groundnut oil
1 finely chopped onion
½ grated apple
75 g (3 oz) ground salted
   peanuts
375 ml (¾ pint) apple
   juice
1 teaspoon turmeric
1 teaspoon salt
black pepper
30 ml (2 tablespoons)
   lemon juice
1 teaspoon sugar

Spinach Mountain

Stir spinach over a low heat until thawed and then continue cooking until all the liquid evaporates. Mix in the raisins, nutmeg, and seasoning. Pile onto a plate and pour cream over the top. Serve at once.

1 carton frozen spinach
   purée
2 teaspoons raisins
nutmeg
3–4 tablespoons heavy
   cream
salt and pepper

Plate 1.

Plate 2.

Plate 3.

Plate 4.

Plate 3.

Plate 4.

Plate 5.

Plate 6.

Plate 7.

Plate 8.

Banana Nut Dessert

Slice bananas and arrange on a large plate. Mix yogurt with all other ingredients and pour over the bananas. Serve chilled.

4 bananas
2 teaspoons flaked almonds
2 teaspoons chopped hazelnuts
2 small cartons plain yogurt
2 teaspoons honey

menu

Asparagus with Cumin Sauce
Sweet Corn Egg Nests with Almond Carrots
Fresh Fruit in Season

Asparagus with Cumin Sauce

Drain asparagus and arrange on individual plates. Mix sour cream, cumin, and seasoning and pour over the tips of the asparagus.

450 g (1 lb) canned asparagus
125 ml (¼ pint) sour cream
2 teaspoons ground cumin
salt and pepper

Sweet Corn Egg Nests

Parboil potatoes for 15 minutes. Peel and slice and lay in buttered individual ovenproof dishes. Sprinkle sweet corn around edges to form a nest. Crack eggs into the center and sprinkle with tarragon and seasoning. Dot with butter. Bake at 220°C/425°F for 15 minutes. **Note:** Use leftover potatoes for a really quick dish.

450 g (1 lb) potatoes
225 g (8 oz) sweet corn
4 eggs
1 teaspoon tarragon
salt and pepper
butter

Almond Carrots

Grate carrots and cook in a little seasoned vegetable stock. When the carrots are cooked, drain and mix with almonds and basil. Dot with butter and serve.

450 g (1 lb) carrots
50 g (2 oz) flaked
   almonds
a little vegetable stock
¼ teaspoon basil
salt and pepper
butter

menu

Cauliflower Colette
Eggs Aurora with Steamed Vegetables
Eastern Apples

Cauliflower Colette

Separate cauliflower into florets and steam for 8 minutes. Drain and allow to cool. Mix curd cheese with rosemary and black pepper and shape into small balls. Arrange in a bowl with cauliflower florets and cover with sour cream mixed with lemon juice and salt.

1 small cauliflower
100 g (4 oz) curd cheese
30 ml (2 tablespoons)
   sour cream
10 ml (2 teaspoons)
   lemon juice
2 teaspoons rosemary
black pepper
salt

Eggs Aurora

Hard boil eggs for 8–10 minutes. Meanwhile sauté finely chopped onions in a little cooking oil. As onions begin to brown, add finely chopped tomato. Continue cooking for 5 minutes. Halve hard-boiled eggs and remove yolks. Mix bread crumbs, parsley, and egg yolks with tomato and onions. Pile mixture into egg whites covering the whole surface. Place under grill for 3–5 minutes to brown.

8 eggs
2 onions
4 tomatoes
75 g (3 oz) bread crumbs
4 tablespoons chopped
   parsley
cooking oil
salt and pepper

Eastern Apples

Peel and slice cooking apples and simmer for 5–8 minutes in a little water. Mash with a fork and add all other ingredients. Serve topped with fresh cream.

450 g (1 lb) cooking apples
6 chopped glacé cherries
1 tablespoon flaked almonds
1 tablespoon raisins
2 tablespoons honey
2 teaspoons candied peel
½ teaspoon cinnamon

menu

Cheese and Semolina Soup
Sesame Potato Patties
with Banana Sauce and Spinach
Fresh Apples and Dates

Cheese and Semolina Soup

Place semolina in a pan with butter and milk. Bring slowly to a boil, stirring all the time. Add salt and pepper and continue cooking for 10 minutes. Add cheese and cook for a further 5 minutes. Sprinkle with nutmeg and serve at once.

2 tablespoons semolina
25 g (1 oz) butter
100 g (4 oz) cheese
1 liter (2 pints) milk
salt and pepper
nutmeg

Sesame Potato Patties

Boil potatoes until soft, drain, and mash with butter. Add ground cooked soya beans, sesame seeds, and seasoning. Mix well and shape into 4 large or 8 small patties. Coat with flour and fry in cooking oil until brown on both sides. Serve with banana sauce and spinach.

700 g (1½ lb) potatoes
350 g (12 oz) cooked soya
  beans
2 teaspoons toasted
  ground sesame seeds
50 g (2 oz) butter
salt and pepper
flour for coating

Banana Sauce

Mash bananas and mix with lemon juice and add a little water if necessary to give a creamy consistency. Finely chop onions and green pepper and fry in cooking oil. Add seasoning, herbs, and banana mixture. Simmer for 20 minutes, blend, and serve.

2 bananas
1 onion
1 small green pepper
juice of 1 lemon
2 tablespoons fresh mint
2 tablespoons fresh
  parsley
garlic salt and black
  pepper
cooking oil

menu

Creole Nut Soup
Cheese Spaghetti Omelette with Watercress
Orange and Grape Salad

Creole Nut Soup

Sauté finely chopped onion and celery in butter until soft. Add tomato paste and flour and season. Blend in peanut butter and add milk gradually, stirring all the time. Bring to boil and add tomato juice. Reheat and serve garnished with sprigs of watercress.

2 medium onions
4 sticks celery
3 tablespoons peanut butter
500 ml (1 pint) tomato juice
25 g (1 oz) butter
2 tablespoons flour
250 ml (½ pint) milk
2 teaspoons tomato purée
salt and pepper
watercress to garnish

Cheese Spaghetti Omelette

Cook spaghetti in boiling salted water. Meanwhile finely chop vegetables and fry in cooking oil until soft. Add drained spaghetti and the well-beaten eggs. Season and leave to set over a fairly low heat. Sprinkle with grated cheese after about 10–15 minutes and finish off under the grill. Serve with watercress.

225 g (8 oz) spaghetti
1 onion
1 small green pepper
100 g (4 oz) mushrooms
2 eggs
100 g (4 oz) Cheddar cheese
salt and pepper
cooking oil
1 bunch watercress

Orange and Grape Salad

Peel and slice oranges and mix with grapes. Grate lemon rind and mix with juice and honey. Sprinkle oranges with a few raisins. Pour on the lemon juice. Leave to chill while the rest of the meal is cooked and eaten.

225 g (8 oz) seedless grapes
2 oranges
1 lemon
1 tablespoon honey
a few raisins

Stuffed Artichoke Hearts
Mushroom Spaghetti Neapolitan
Cheese Board

Stuffed Artichoke Hearts

Cook peas in boiling salted water. Drain and allow to cool. Arrange hearts on individual plates and stuff with peas, allowing them to overflow onto the plate. Garnish with tomato slices. Sprinkle with tarragon and pour 2 tablespoons of dressing over each serving.

1 can artichoke hearts
225 g (8 oz) frozen or
  fresh peas
125 ml (¼ pint) oil and
  vinegar dressing
1 teaspoon tarragon
2 tomatoes
salt and pepper

Mushroom Spaghetti Neapolitan

Cook spaghetti in boiling salted water for about 15 minutes. Meanwhile fry mushrooms very gently in a little cooking oil. In another pan fry finely sliced onions until transparent. Add chopped tomatoes, tomato paste, herbs, and seasoning. Cover with stock and simmer for 20 minutes until thick. Toss spaghetti in cream with mushrooms and serve topped with tomato sauce. Sprinkle with Parmesan to taste.

350 g (12 oz) spaghetti
225 g (8 oz) mushrooms
700 g (1½ lb) tomatoes
2 onions
250 ml (½ pint) water
1 tablespoon tomato
  paste
1 teaspoon oregano
garlic salt and black
  pepper
cooking oil
125 ml (¼ pint) heavy
  cream
Parmesan cheese

98

Jerusalem Artichoke Soup
Egg and Potato Tortilla with Buttered Green Beans
Fresh Fruit in Season

Jerusalem Artichoke Soup

Slice leeks and fry in a little cooking oil. Scrub artichokes and potato and remove any black bits. Slice and add to leeks. Cover with milk and stock and add herbs and seasoning. Bring to boil and simmer for 20 minutes. Serve as it is or quickly pass through a mouli. Sprinkle with chopped parsley to garnish.

450 g (1 lb) Jerusalem artichokes
2 leeks
1 large potato
250 ml (½ pint) vegetable stock
250 ml (½ pint) milk
salt and pepper
cooking oil
1 bay leaf
¼ teaspoon marjoram
chopped parsley

Egg and Potato Tortilla

Dice vegetables finely and fry gently in cooking oil for about 5 minutes. Beat eggs, season, and pour over the vegetables. Turn the heat down low and leave to set for about 10 minutes. Turn over with a fish slicer and cook for a further 10 minutes. Serve with buttered green beans.

3 potatoes
1 onion
1 tomato
½ green pepper
2 zucchini if available
4 eggs
salt and pepper
cooking oil

Quick Snacks

Scramble Surprise

Place nuts in a pan with water and Marmite. Cook for 15 minutes until thick, stirring from time to time. Beat eggs with seasoning and add to nut mixture. Continue stirring over a medium heat until scrambled. Toast bread and serve scrambled eggs on the toast, topped with two slices of tomato and some fresh parsley.

4 eggs
50 g (2 oz) ground
   peanuts
125 ml (¼ pint) water
½ teaspoon Marmite or
   yeast extract
salt and pepper
4 slices whole meal bread
2 tomatoes
parsley

Greek Salad*

Coarsely chop lettuce, tomatoes, cucumber, and other salad in season. Arrange in bowls with the olives. Mix oil and vinegar with herbs and black pepper and pour over the salads. Flake the cheese on the top. Serve with hot Greek bread.

½ lettuce
4 tomatoes
10 cm (4 in) cucumber
12 black olives
watercress, radishes,
   spring onions in season
225 g (8 oz) Feta cheese
1 teaspoon thyme
½ teaspoon oregano
60 ml (4 tablespoons)
   olive oil
15–30 ml (1–2
   tablespoons) vinegar
black pepper

*See Plate 1.

Welsh Rarebit on Toast

Make a thick roux sauce with butter, flour, and beer. Add cheese and stir well. Next add mustard, Worcestershire sauce, and Cayenne pepper to taste. Toast and butter the bread and spread generously with the rarebit mixture and grill quickly until brown.

Note: This mixture keeps for considerable time in a covered container in the refrigerator.

4 large slices whole wheat bread
25 g (1 oz) butter
25 g (1 oz) flour
250 ml (8 oz) beer
100 g (4 oz) grated cheese
½–1 teaspoon mustard
Worcestershire sauce
Cayenne pepper

Nut Rarebit on Toast

Make a thickish roux sauce with the butter, flour, beer, and milk. Add cheese and nuts and stir well. Add Worcestershire sauce and Cayenne pepper to taste. Toast bread and butter. Spread the rarebit mixture generously over the toast and place under the grill until brown.

4 large slices whole wheat bread
25 g (1 oz) butter
25 g (1 oz) flour
125 ml (¼ pint) beer
125 ml (¼ pint) milk
50 g (2 oz) cheese
50 g (2 oz) ground roast nuts (peanuts, almonds, hazelnuts)
Worcestershire sauce
Cayenne pepper

Deviled Mushrooms on Toast

Gently fry whole mushrooms on both sides in butter. Toast bread and place one mushroom on each slice. Mix all other ingredients and spoon over the mushrooms. Quickly place under the grill and cook for 3–4 minutes.

225 g (8 oz) large field mushrooms (4)
4 slices whole wheat bread
30 ml (2 tablespoons) heavy cream
5 ml (1 teaspoon) Worcestershire sauce
5 ml (1 teaspoon) tomato ketchup
1 teaspoon French mustard
25 g (1 oz) butter
salt and pepper

Chili Cheese Spread on Toast

Empty can of beans into a pan and mash with a fork. Heat through. Meanwhile toast and butter the bread. Remove bean mixture from the heat and add cheese and marjoram and more chili powder if desired. Spread over the toast and place under the grill for 2–3 minutes.

1 small can beans in chili sauce
100 g (4 oz) cheese
2 teaspoons marjoram
extra chili powder as required
4 large slices whole wheat bread

Omelette Provençale

Finely chop onion and garlic. Fry in butter until transparent. Add chopped tomatoes and peppers and tomato paste. Sprinkle with a little flour. Season and stir well. Allow to cook for about 15 minutes until the vegetables are tender. Beat eggs and milk and make either 1 large or 4 small omelettes. Fill with provençale vegetable mixture.

8 eggs
45 ml (3 tablespoons) milk
water
salt and pepper

Filling
2 onions
2 tomatoes
1 green pepper
1 clove garlic
1 teaspoon tomato paste
a little flour
salt and pepper
butter

Crunchy Omelette Surprise

Finely chop mushrooms and sauté in cooking oil. When they are soft, add corn flour and stir in sufficient milk to give a thick creamy consistency. Season and cook for 5 minutes. Beat eggs together and add flaked almonds, finely chopped spring onions, and seasoning. Make an omelette with the egg mixture and fill with mushroom sauce.

8 eggs
25 g (1 oz) flaked
  almonds
4 spring onions
milk
salt and pepper
cooking oil

Filling
225 g (8 oz) mushrooms
1 tablespoon corn flour
milk
salt and pepper
cooking oil

Marmite Crumpets

Spread the underside of the crumpets with a little butter and place these on a baking sheet. Blend remaining butter with the Marmite and spread on top of the crumpets. Separate the yolk from the white, add the yolk to the grated cheese. Stiffly whisk the egg white and fold into the mixture with a little pepper. Divide between the crumpets. Cook in a moderate oven at 180°C/350°F for about 20 minutes.

4 crumpets
50 g (2 oz) butter
1 level teaspoon Marmite
  or yeast extract
50 g (2 oz) Cheddar
  cheese, grated
1 egg
pepper

Corn Potato Cake

Grate potatoes and finely chop onion and mix with sweet corn, flour, eggs, and seasoning. Fry in cooking oil on one side for 5–8 minutes. Turn over and fry on the other side. Serve garnished with watercress.

3 potatoes
2 onions
1 small 215 g (7½ oz) can
  sweet corn
2 tablespoons plain flour
2 eggs
salt and pepper
cooking oil
watercress

Cheese and Nut Patties

Cook potatoes and then peel and mash with cottage cheese and nuts. Finely chop chives and spring onions and add to the mixture. Season and roll in bread crumbs. Fry on both sides in cooking oil.

700 g (1½ lb) potatoes
350 g (12 oz) cottage cheese
75 g (3 oz) ground peanuts
fresh chives or spring onions
salt and pepper
50 g (2 oz) toasted bread crumbs
cooking oil

Deviled Beans on Toast

Finely slice onion and fry in a small pan in cooking oil. Add tomato paste, mustard, Worcestershire sauce, soya sauce, and vinegar. Bring to the boil and add contents of can of beans. Toast bread, butter, and spread the beans on top.

425 g (15 oz) can Boston baked beans
1 large onion
2 tablespoons tomato paste
45 ml (3 tablespoons) vinegar
30 ml (2 tablespoons) soya sauce
5 ml (1 teaspoon) Worcestershire sauce
1 teaspoon English mustard
cooking oil
salt and pepper
4 slices whole meal bread

Breakfast and 8 Brunches

Breakfast is perhaps the most important meal of the day yet it is sadly neglected by many people. Ideally it should contain some of all the essential nutrients and account for about 25% of all food taken during the day.

Breakfast is even more important for growing children, so do make sure that they have something to eat before leaving for school. A glass of milk with the meal provides extra protein, as well as calcium and other nutrients. Fruit or orange juice at breakfast is also a good idea as it provides vitamin C to help fight infection and to help in the assimilation of iron in cereals.

Good old-fashioned porridge served with milk and honey is an excellent start to the day as it is a good source of both carbohydrates for energy and protein for body building. Muesli is another all-in-one dish that is popular at breakfast time. If you have a heavy day ahead, add a boiled egg and a slice of toast to the menu and you should have plenty of energy to last until lunchtime.

Muesli was originally developed by Dr. Bircher-Benner at his clinic in Switzerland to encourage the consumption of raw foods and particularly fruit. Today there are many variations on the muesli theme, but in the original recipe the emphasis was on the fruit content rather than the cereals. Muesli doesn't take long to make. The cereals are soaked in water overnight and the fruit added just before serving.

With a little imagination you can easily make your own variations. Try mixing different whole grain cereals with the oats—some companies sell ready mixed muesli bases containing four or five different grains. Use whatever fresh fruit is in season; black currants, plums, and mashed bananas are particularly good. Or use dried fruits in the winter.

Here is Dr. Bircher-Benner's original recipe:

Apple Muesli

Mix lemon juice and condensed milk to a smooth cream. Add oats and stir thoroughly. Wash apples, wipe with a cloth, and remove tops, stalks, and any blemishes. Grate apple into oat mixture, stirring frequently to prevent discoloring. Sprinkle nuts over finished dish and serve at once.

4 level tablespoons rolled oats soaked for 12 hours in 180 ml (12 tablespoons) of water

60 ml (4 tablespoons) lemon juice

60 ml (4 tablespoons) sweetened condensed milk

4 large apples

4 tablespoons grated hazelnuts or almonds

Winter Muesli Mix with Yogurt

Mix muesli base with honey and yogurt and add raisins and walnuts. Grate pears, apples, and a little orange rind into the mixture and stir well. Finally, squeeze the orange and add to the muesli. Serve at once.

4 tablespoons mixed cereal base soaked overnight in 180 ml (12 tablespoons) water
1 tablespoon raisins
2 tablespoons chopped walnuts
2 pears
2 apples
1 orange
1 teaspoon honey
125 ml (¼ pint) carton plain yogurt

Summer Fruit Muesli

Mix muesli base with cream and almonds. Finely chop melon and add to the muesli mixture. Serve sprinkled with fresh raspberries.

4 tablespoons mixed cereal base soaked overnight in 180 ml (12 tablespoons) water
2 tablespoons chopped almonds
60 ml (4 tablespoons) heavy cream
½ small melon
150 g (6 oz) fresh raspberries

Citrus Oats

Mix oats with yogurt and honey and grate a little orange rind into the mixture. Peel oranges and grapefruit and chop segments. Mix with oats and serve at once.

4 tablespoons rolled oats soaked overnight in 180 ml (12 tablespoons) water
2 grapefruit
2 oranges
125 ml (¼ pint) carton plain yogurt
1 teaspoon honey

One of the reasons why so many people skip breakfast is that they believe it takes too long to get ready. But this doesn't have to be the case. Some of the preparation can be done the night before. For example, eggs for scrambling can be beaten up the night before and stored in a plastic container in the refrigerator; extra rice or potatoes can be cooked at dinner time and kept for the following morning; and pancakes can be mixed and even made the day before.

Extra protein is soon added to a standard orange juice, coffee, and toast breakfast by spreading the toast with peanut butter or cottage cheese, or grilling it with grated cheese and tomato.

Coddled eggs are quick and easy if you have some egg coddlers—they are made by most leading dishware manufacturers. Grease the coddlers well and break an egg into the bottom of each. Then add a knob of butter and any of the following flavorings: slices of tomato, finely chopped green pepper or mushrooms, mixed herbs, ground cumin, or toasted sesame seed, or left-over sauces. Screw down the lid and coddle eggs in a pan of boiling water for about 5–6 minutes until they are set. You can eat the eggs straight from the coddler or turn the eggs onto buttered toast.

The Dutch have the quick nutritious breakfast down to a fine art, and it might be worth taking a tip or two from them. They serve a variety of different kinds of bread—you could experiment with rye bread, granary bread, oat plait (see Chapter 9), or crisp breads of various kinds—with a selection of thinly sliced cheeses and hard-boiled eggs.

Below are 8 really quick recipes, followed by a selection of recipes for the weekend when you have more time or when breakfast becomes brunch.

Eggy Bread and Tomatoes

Beat the eggs with a fork and season. Cut the slices of bread in half. Dip them in the egg mixture and fry in hot butter. Slice the tomatoes in half and dot with butter. Place under a hot grill. Service the tomato on slices of eggy bread.

4 large slices bread
2 eggs
salt and pepper
4 large tomatoes
butter

Indian Toast

Mix cheese, chutney, and curry powder to a thick paste. Slice tomatoes. Grill bread on both sides and then cover with sliced tomatoes and then the cheese mixture. Place under the grill for 3–4 minutes until the cheese is bubbly.

4 large slices bread
2 tablespoons chutney
100 g (4 oz) grated cheese
4 tomatoes
1 teaspoon curry powder

Egg and Potato Pancake

Chop boiled eggs and mix with mashed potato and French mustard. Season and fry in melted butter until the underside is browned. Turn over with a fish slice and brown the second side.

450 g (1 lb) leftover
   mashed potato
4 hard-boiled eggs
1 tablespoon French
   mustard
25 g (1 oz) butter
2 tablespoons chopped
   parsley
salt and pepper

Country Scramble

Finely chop mushrooms and tomatoes and mix with eggs. Heat milk and butter in a pan and add egg mixture. Season and scramble until cooked. Serve on toast.

6 eggs
50 g (2 oz) mushrooms
3 small tomatoes
25 g (1 oz) butter
90 ml (6 tablespoons)
   milk
salt and pepper
4 slices toast

Sunshine Crumpets

Poach eggs until set. Grill crumpets and spread with butter and tomato ketchup. Place an egg on top of each crumpet and season. Sprinkle with grated cheese and grill until the cheese melts.

4 crumpets
4 eggs
1 tablespoon tomato ketchup
100 g (4 oz) grated cheese
butter
salt and pepper

Stuffed Mushrooms

Wash the mushrooms and quickly fry in butter. When they are partially cooked, remove from frying pan and place in a heatproof dish. Make bread crumbs from the bread and mix with finely chopped spring onions, cheese, tomato paste, honey, herbs, and seasoning and moisten with stock. Pile on top of the mushrooms. Dot with butter and bake under the grill for about 5 minutes.

4 large field mushrooms

Stuffing
4 spring onions
2 slices bread
50 g (2 oz) cheese
2 teaspoons tomato paste
1 teaspoon honey
½ teaspoon marjoram
salt and pepper
stock
butter

Bean
and Potato Lyonnaise

Slice onion and fry in cooking oil until transparent. Slice potato and add to the onion. Fry for 5 minutes and add beans. Continue to fry gently until all ingredients are heated through. Sprinkle with marjoram and seasoning and add tomato paste mixed with a little water to give a creamy consistency. Toss vegetables in the tomato mixture until really hot. Serve at once.

350 g (12 oz) boiled potatoes
150 g (6 oz) cooked beans (soya, haricot, or blackeye)
1 large onion
1 tablespoon tomato paste
1 teaspoon marjoram
salt and pepper
a little water
cooking oil

Egg Bolognaise

Empty the contents of the can of spaghetti into a nonstick frying pan. Make four hollows in the spaghetti and break an egg into each hollow. Sprinkle grated cheese over the top and cook over a low heat until the eggs are set. Finish off under the grill.

1 large can or jar
spaghetti in tomato sauce
4 eggs
50 g (2 oz) grated cheese

Cheesy Rice
with Mushrooms

Finely chop onion and celery and fry in a little butter. Cook rice in boiling salted water for about 15–20 minutes. When cooked, drain and mix in cheese and vegetables. Season to taste and add a little sage. Wash mushrooms and dot with butter. Grill until soft and serve with cheesy rice.

225 g (8 oz) rice
100 g (4 oz) grated cheese
1 small onion
1 stick celery
¼ teaspoon sage
salt and pepper
100 g (4 oz) button
  mushrooms
butter

Brunch Rosti

Grate onions and potatoes and mix with beaten egg, Marmite, and flour. Add seasoning and fry in hot cooking oil for 8–10 minutes. Turn over and cook the second side for a further 8–10 minutes. Serve garnished with sliced tomatoes.

700 g (1½ lb) potatoes
2 onions
2 eggs
1 teaspoon Marmite or
  yeast extract
1 tablespoon plain flour
salt and pepper
cooking oil
2 tomatoes

Savory Mushroom Pancakes

Mix flour with egg and half the milk and beat well. Add remaining milk and seasoning. Leave to stand. Finely chop mushrooms and fry in butter for 6–8 minutes. Mix cornflour with a little milk and then add remaining milk and seasoning. Pour over the mushrooms and bring to boil, stirring all the time. When the mixture has thickened, simmer for a further 10 minutes. Make 8 small pancakes with the pancake mixture and fill with mushroom filling.

Pancakes
75 g (3 oz) flour
175 ml (7 fl. oz) milk
1 egg
salt

Filling
225 g (8 oz) mushrooms
1 tablespoon corn flour
350 ml (14 fl. oz) milk
butter
salt and pepper

Apricot Brunch Bread

Soak apricots overnight, drain, and chop. Soak all-bran in milk. Cream butter and sugar and gradually beat in the eggs. Fold in flour and then stir in apricots, chopped hazelnuts, and all-bran. Place the mixture in a greased 450 g (1 lb) bread pan and bake at 180°C/350°F for 1–1¼ hours. Turn out and serve warm or cold with butter.

100 g (4 oz) self-raising
   flour
25 g (1 oz) soya flour
50 g (2 oz) all-bran
100 g (4 oz) butter
100 g (4 oz) soft brown
   sugar
50 g (2 oz) chopped
   hazelnuts
100 g (4 oz) dried
   apricots
125 ml (¼ pint) milk
2 eggs

African Kedgeree

Cook rice in boiling salted water and drain. Chop hard-boiled eggs and mix with rice. Add oregano and peanuts. Melt butter in a pan with the Marmite. Add the rice mixture and toss over the heat with a fork until well heated through. Pile onto a serving dish and garnish with chopped parsley.

225 g (8 oz) rice
4 hard-boiled eggs
50 g (2 oz) roast peanuts
1 teaspoon Marmite or
   yeast extract
½ teaspoon oregano
50 g (2 oz) butter
chopped parsley

Lentil Risotto with Cheesy Tomatoes

Finely slice onions and fry in cooking oil with cumin seed for 5 minutes. Add rice and lentils and fry for a further 2–3 minutes. Add stock and seasoning and bring to boil. Simmer until all the liquid is taken up— about 35–40 minutes. Meanwhile halve tomatoes and pile up with cheese. Place under a hot grill until the cheese begins to brown. Serve with lentil risotto.

150 g (6 oz) long grain rice
100 g (4 oz) lentils
2 onions
1 teaspoon ground cumin seed
625 ml (1¼ pints) vegetable stock
cooking oil
4 tomatoes
50 g (2 oz) grated cheese
salt and pepper

Buckwheat Pancakes

Mix sugar and yeast with a little warm water and leave until it goes creamy. Add remaining warm water and whisk in the buckwheat flour. Leave to stand in a warm place until the mixture is full of bubbles. Whisk in a beaten egg and make 8 small pancakes. Serve with lemon and honey.

1 teaspoon sugar
half 12½ g (½ oz) package dried yeast
250 ml (½ pint) warm water
100 g (4 oz) buckwheat flour
1 egg
salt and pepper
lemon juice and honey

Whole Meal Puffs

Separate eggs and beat yolks till really stiff and pale yellow in color. Add milk and flour alternately, beating all the time. Add salt to egg whites and beat until really stiff. Fold egg whites into batter. Spoon into greased muffin pans and bake at 230°C/450°F for 30 minutes.

4 eggs
500 ml (1 pint) milk
5 tablespoons whole meal flour
1 teaspoon salt

Packed Lunches and Picnics 9

Too often packed lunches are regarded as just a stopgap between breakfast in the morning and a cooked meal in the evening. Yet many people, including growing children, have to eat them every day. Picnics, too, are often hastily thrown together without much thought for their food value.

There is, in fact, no real reason why packed lunches and picnics shouldn't be as healthy and appetizing as any other meal. The same guidelines apply, and provided that at least one item is chosen from each of the four groups of food outlined in Chapter 3, the meal will be a nutritious one. Add some extra protein if the packed lunch is for growing children and cut down on the carbohydrates if it is for a sedentary worker.

Very often the main problem with packed lunches is the time required to get them together. So if you are making packed lunches every day, here are a few ideas to help cut down the preparation time in the morning.

1) Make salads the night before and keep in the refrigerator in airtight plastic containers. They will be just as crisp and crunchy at lunchtime the following day. Do not add dressing to green salad or mushrooms, but add lemon juice and a very little oil to chopped or grated root vegetables.

2) Make double or triple batches of sandwich fillings and store in the refrigerator or freezer in airtight containers to use later in the week or month.

114

3) Make up batches of sandwiches and freeze in individual wrappings. If they are removed in the morning, they will be thawed and fresh at lunchtime. Avoid hard-boiled eggs or salad fillings if the sandwiches are going in the freezer. Also freeze pies and quiches in individual portions, and you have an instant choice for lunch.

4) Keep margarine or delicatessan containers and use to pack salad items, fruit salad, or pâté. They are convenient and save a lot of mess.

5) Include fresh fruit, tomatoes, yogurt, cottage cheese, or milk. They are all nutritious and require little or no preparation on your part.

6) Add a thermos of hot or cold soup depending on the season.

Keeping up the interest and variety is the second major problem for regular packed-lunch eaters. Sandwiches day in and day out can become extremely boring, however exotic the fillings. So alternate sandwiches with homemade pies, pâté, and rolls or quiche. Change the accompanying salads and use different kinds of bread on the sandwich days.

Here are some ideas for different sandwich fillings and double-decker sandwiches. Quantities vary depending on the number of people you are catering for and the size of their appetites. As a rough guide, allow about 50 g (2 oz) cheese, 1 egg or 50 g (2 oz) pâté or spread, together with salad items or garnish for a sandwich made from a standard size loaf. These ideas are followed by some recipes for picnics.

Sandwich fillings

Finely chopped hard-boiled eggs mixed with finely chopped onion, mint, and a little mayonnaise.

Grated Cheddar cheese mixed with grated carrot and black pepper.

Ground roast peanuts mixed with mayonnaise and chopped watercress.

Grated Cheshire cheese mixed with finely chopped celery, fennel seed, and a little natural yogurt.

Scrambled egg mixed with chopped chives and cumin seed.

Peanut butter mixed with finely chopped shallots, fresh mixed herbs, a little honey, and lemon juice.

Cottage cheese mixed with chopped green pepper and flaked almonds.

Finely chopped hard-boiled egg mixed with chopped walnuts, mayonnaise, and cress.

Cream cheese mixed with Marmite and watercress.

Ground cooked soya beans mixed with Marmite, chopped tomatoes, and herbs.

Cream cheese mixed with chopped stuffed olives, gherkins, and garlic salt.

Mexican double decker

First Layer
Scrambled egg and mixed herbs with sliced tomato.

Second Layer
Sliced cucumber, watercress, chopped green and red pepper, and mayonnaise mixed with a little chilli powder.

Cheese and walnut decker

First Layer
Grated Cheddar cheese mixed with a little mayonnaise and chopped walnuts.

Second Layer
Watercress with chopped radishes and spring onions.

Beet and coleslaw club

First Layer
American coleslaw (see Chapter 6 under Salad Medley).

Second Layer
Sliced beetroot and grated Edam cheese.

Nutty Parisian

First Layer
Scramble Surprise (see Chapter 7 under Quick Snacks)
and sliced tomatoes.

Second Layer
Lettuce, finely sliced raw onion, and a thin slice of
Cheddar cheese.

Peanut decker

First Layer
Peanut butter and sliced pickled cucumber.

Second Layer
Sliced beetroot and watercress.

Yorkshire filler

First Layer
Grated Wensleydale cheese.

Second Layer
Sliced apples, cucumber, and mayonnaise.

Barbecued Cheese Filling

Blend all ingredients adding sufficient milk to give a creamy consistency. Place in the refrigerator and use any time during the following week. This quantity is sufficient for 4–6 sandwiches. Garnish with watercress, parsley, or tomato slices.

75 g (3 oz) cream cheese
50 g (2 oz) butter
75 g (3 oz) red Leicester cheese
15 ml (1 tablespoon) Worcestershire sauce
1 teaspoon tomato paste
milk
salt and pepper

Oriental Spread

Grate cheese and mix with mashed bananas and chopped dates. Season and add chutney to give a smooth consistency. This quantity is sufficient for 4–6 sandwiches. Garnish with watercress, cress, or cucumber slices.

150 g (6 oz) Cheddar cheese
2 bananas
8 dates
2 tablespoons chutney
salt and pepper

Mexican Quiche

Make pastry by rubbing fat into flour and salt and bind with water. Roll out and line a 20 cm (8 in) flan pan. Slice the onion and green pepper and simmer in a little water for 8–10 minutes. Drain well and mix with drained sweet corn. Arrange in the base of the flan. Mix grated cheese with beaten eggs, cream, and seasonings and pour over the vegetables. Bake at 200°C/400°F for 50 minutes to 1 hour until the quiche is set and lightly browned on the top.

Pastry
100 g (4 oz) plain flour
50 g (2 oz) butter
salt
water

Filling
3 eggs
75 g (3 oz) cheese
1 small green pepper
1 small can sweet corn or Mexicorn
1 small onion
125 ml (¼ pint) reg. cream
salt and pepper

Chestnut Picnic Pie

Rub fat into flour and salt and bind with beaten egg. Roll out and line a 20 cm (8 in) flan pan, retaining sufficient pastry to make a lid. Boil potatoes and hard boil one of the eggs. Drain chestnuts. Slice cooked potatoes, hard-boiled egg, and chestnuts and arrange in layers on the pastry base. Beat the remaining two eggs with the cream and pour over the vegetables. Top with the pastry lid and bake at 200°C/400°F for 50 minutes to 1 hour.

Pastry
150 g (6 oz) plain flour
75 g (3 oz) butter
salt
beaten egg

Filling
225 g (8 oz) potatoes
3 eggs
285 g (10 oz) can whole
  chestnuts
125 ml (¼ pint) cream
1 teaspoon marjoram
salt and pepper

Leicestershire Picnic Roll

Chop Stilton and mix with walnuts and mayonnaise. Cut the French bread in half lengthways, taking care not to cut all the way through at the back of the loaf. Scoop out some of the dough from the center and spread each half of the loaf with the Stilton mixture. Lay the watercress down the center of the loaf. Close up the two halves and wrap in foil to keep fresh. Cut into 8 chunks to serve.

225 g (8 oz) Stilton cheese
50 g (2 oz) chopped
  walnuts
30 ml (2 tablespoons)
  mayonnaise
1 bunch watercress
salt and pepper
35 cm (14 in) French
  bread

Queensway Pasties

Finely chop mushrooms and fry in a little butter until soft. Drain well and mix with grated potatoes and finely chopped onions. Add beaten egg, flour, thyme, and seasoning and mix well. Make pastry by rubbing fat into flour and salt and binding with beaten egg, retaining any unused egg to glaze the finished pasties. Roll out the pastry and cut into 4 oval shapes. Place a quarter of the filling in each one and join the pastry over the top, pinching it together between the finger and thumb. Glaze with beaten egg and place on a greased baking pan. Bake at 200°C/400°F for 30–35 minutes.

Pastry
150 g (6 oz) plain flour
75 g (3 oz) butter
salt
beaten egg

Filling
225 g (8 oz) mushrooms
2 potatoes
2 small onions
1 egg
1 tablespoon plain flour
1 teaspoon thyme
salt and pepper
butter

Whitbourne Surprise Eggs

Hard boil eggs and allow to cool. Halve the eggs and remove the yolks. Mix the yolks with mayonnaise and herbs and stuff back into the egg whites. Push the two halves together to reform whole eggs. Dissolve the agar-agar in boiling water into which the Marmite has been mixed. Place the eggs in small molds and surround with chopped gherkin. Pour on the agar-agar mixture and leave to set in a cool place.

4 eggs
1 teaspoon mayonnaise
½ teaspoon mixed herbs
500 ml (1 pint) water
1 teaspoon Marmite or
   yeast extract
3 teaspoons agar-agar
1 large gherkin

*See Plate 7 (top).

Egg and Tomato Galantine

Cook rice in boiling salted water. Finely chop onion, celery, and tomato and fry gently in cooking oil for 5 minutes. Drain cooked rice and mix with bread crumbs and fried vegetables. Add ground almonds, soya flour, tomato paste, and herbs. Season and bind with beaten eggs. Press half the mixture into a greased 450 g (1 lb) bread pan and place the hard-boiled eggs on the top. Cover with the remaining mixture and press down. Bake at 190°C/375°F for 1 hour. Allow to cool for 5 minutes and then turn out. Leave till really cold. Serve cut into slices with one of the picnic salads.

2 hard-boiled eggs
100 g (4 oz) rice
50 g (2 oz) bread crumbs
2 sticks celery
2 onions
3 tomatoes
50 g (2 oz) ground almonds
2 tablespoons tomato paste
1 tablespoon soya flour
2 eggs
½ teaspoon rosemary
1 teaspoon oregano
salt and pepper
cooking oil

St. Christopher Savory Roll

Grate cheese and finely chop onions. Mix with tomato paste and seasoning. Rub fat into flour and salt to make the pastry and bind with water. Roll out and spread the cheese mixture all over the pastry, leaving a small margin clear around the edges. Roll up the pastry and filling rather like a flattish Swiss roll. Place on a greased baking tray in a slightly curved shape. Cut across the roll, leaving the pastry uncut at the side to make about 12 sections. Twist each section to lie on its side exposing the Swiss roll effect. Bake at 200°C/400°F for about 25–30 minutes.

Pastry
150 g (6 oz) plain flour
75 g (3 oz) butter
salt
water

Filling
150 g (6 oz) cheese
2 onions
2 tablespoons tomato paste
salt and pepper

Hazelnut Terrine en Croûte*

Chop onions, celery, and green pepper and mix with nuts, bread crumbs, herbs, and seasoning. Bind with beaten eggs. Make pastry by rubbing fat into flour and salt and binding with beaten egg. Retain remaining beaten egg to glaze the finished croûte. Roll out three-quarters of the pastry and place the terrine mixture down the center of the pastry. Wrap the pastry around the mixture, sealing on the top and at each end. Roll out remaining pastry and cut out leaf shapes. Use a knife to mark out center ribs and veins and arrange on top of the roll to mask the join. Press down with a little water on the joining surfaces and brush with beaten egg. Bake at 200°C/400°F for 45–50 minutes until the pastry is crisp and lightly browned. Allow to cool on a wire tray.

Pastry
225 g (8 oz) plain flour
75 g (3 oz) butter
2 eggs
salt

Filling
2 onions
½ green pepper
100 g (4 oz) bread crumbs
75 g (3 oz) hazelnuts
3 sticks celery
2 eggs
1 teaspoon marjoram
½ teaspoon ground cumin seed
1 teaspoon freshly chopped sage
salt and pepper

Savory French Roll

Cut French bread in half lengthways, but do not cut all the way through. Hollow out the center and butter. Finely chop gherkins and chives or spring onions and mix with all other ingredients. Press into the center of the loaf and close up. Wrap in foil or plastic wrap and cut into 8 chunks for serving.

225 g (8 oz) cottage cheese
100 g (4 oz) ground cooked soya beans
3 pickled gherkins
15 ml (1 tablespoon) mayonnaise
1 teaspoon marjoram
1 bunch chives or 6 spring onions
salt and pepper
35 cm (14 in) French bread

*See Plate 7 (bottom).

Date and Nut Quiche

Make pastry by rubbing fat into flour and salt and binding with water. Roll out and line a 20 cm [8 in] flan plan. Grate cheese and mix with beaten eggs, nuts, cream, and seasoning. Stone and chop the dates and place in the base of the flan. Pour over the egg and cheese mixture and add a little milk if the mixture is not sufficient. Fork in, taking care not to pierce the pastry base. Bake at 200°C/400°F for about 50 minutes to 1 hour until the quiche is set and lightly browned on top.

Pastry
100 g (4 oz) plain flour
50 g (2 oz) butter
salt
water

Filling
3 eggs
100 g (4 oz) cheese
50 g (2 oz) mixed ground
  nuts
100 g (4 oz) dates
125 ml (¼ pint) reg.
  cream
milk
salt and pepper

Mixed Picnic Salad

Finely dice all vegetables and mix with lemon juice. If stored in an airtight plastic container, the salad will keep in good condition overnight. Serve with fresh watercress and whole tomatoes.

1 small head fennel
2 carrots
¼ small cucumber
2 sticks celery
8 radishes
4 spring onions
juice of 1 lemon

Egg Waldorf Salad

Chop eggs, apples, and celery and mix with walnuts, mayonnaise, seasoning, and a little ground cumin seed. Place in a plastic container and keep as cool as possible.

4 hard-boiled eggs
2 eating apples
4 sticks celery
25 g (1 oz) chopped
  walnuts
10 ml (2 teaspoons)
  mayonnaise
salt and pepper
ground cumin seed

Beanshoot Salad

Shred carrots and mix with raisins and dressing. Cut cucumber into thin sticks and add to the carrots. Keep in the refrigerator until needed. Take the beanshoots separately and mix with carrots and cucumber mixture just before serving.

225 g (8 oz) beanshoots
1 pickled cucumber
2 carrots
1 tablespoon raisins
30 ml (2 tablespoons) oil
  and vinegar dressing

Celeriac Salad

Peel celeriac and slice finely. Cut each slice into very thin sticks and mix with mayonnaise and seasoning. Leave to stand overnight in the refrigerator in a covered container. Serve at lunchtime the following day.

1 large celeriac
60 ml (4 tablespoons)
  mayonnaise
salt and pepper

Buckwheat Cheese Biscuits

Mix buckwheat and plain flour. Add salt and rub in the fat. Add grated cheese and bind with water. Roll out thinly and cut into rounds. Bake on a greased tray at 200°C/400°F for 15–20 minutes.

50 g (2 oz) buckwheat
  flour
50 g (2 oz) plain flour
50 g (2 oz) butter
50 g (2 oz) grated cheese
salt and pepper
water

Oatmeal Picnic Bread

Mix yeast with a little of the warm water and leave to stand in a warm place for 5 minutes. Mix flour, oats, and salt. Add oil, yeast, milk, and water. Mix well and then knead for 5–8 minutes until the dough is smooth and elastic. Shape into a long roll and cut a pattern on the top with a sharp knife. Place on a greased baking pan and cover with a cloth. Leave to rise for 1 hour in a warm place. Then bake at 230°C/450°F for ½ hour.

50 g (2 oz) oatmeal
50 g (2 oz) rolled oats
350 g (12 oz) plain flour
12½ g (½ oz) dried yeast
125 ml (¼ pint) warm
  water
125 ml (¼ pint) warm
  milk
30 ml (2 tablespoons)
  salad oil
salt

Marmalade Fruit Loaf

Beat egg and mix with milk, oil, treacle, syrup, and marmalade. Mix flour and raisins and add liquid mixture. The result should be a fairly stiff dough. Spoon into a well-greased 450 g (1 lb) pan and bake at 180°C/350°F for 1 hour.

225 g (8 oz) self-raising flour
50 g (2 oz) raisins
1 tablespoon marmalade
1 tablespoon black treacle
1 tablespoon golden syrup
1 tablespoon corn oil
200 ml (4 fl. oz) milk
1 egg

Apple Turnovers

Rub fat into flour and salt to make pastry and bind with water. Roll out and cut into 4 oval shapes. Peel and slice the cooking apples and arrange half an apple on each oval. Add raisins and orange rind and sugar if desired. Fold the pastry over the apples and pinch at the side to seal. Place on a greased baking tray and bake at 200°C/400°F for 25–30 minutes.

Pastry
150 g (6 oz) plain flour
75 g (3 oz) butter
salt
water

Filling
2 cooking apples
2 tablespoons seedless raisins
orange rind
a little sugar (optional)

Dinner Parties, Formal and Informal 10

menu

Spinach Gnocchi
Ratatouille Roulade
with New Potatoes and Broccoli
Apple, Date, and Oatmeal Pie with Cream

Spinach Gnocchi

Thaw spinach in a pan with a very little butter and cook for a few minutes. Drain and retain liquid. Make up to 375 ml (¾ pint) with milk. Place in a pan with butter and semolina and bring to a boil, stirring all the time. Add spinach and salt and continue cooking for 10–15 minutes. Stir from time to time. Pour into a bowl and allow to cool.

Meanwhile make a roux sauce with the butter, flour, and milk and stir in the cream cheese and seasoning. Place two rounded tablespoons of the gnocchi mixture into small individual ovenproof dishes and cover with sauce. Sprinkle with Parmesan and brown in the oven for 15–20 minutes at 200°C/400°F.

Gnocchi
225 g (8 oz) block frozen
  chopped spinach
40 g (1½ oz) semolina
25 g (1 oz) butter
375 ml (¾ pint) milk and
  juice from spinach
salt

Sauce
25 g (1 oz) butter
25 g (1 oz) flour
375 ml (¾ pint) milk
100 g (4 oz) cream cheese
2 tablespoons Parmesan
  cheese
salt and pepper
¼ teaspoon celery seed
  or celery salt

126

Ratatouille Roulade

Slice all vegetables and fry in a little cooking oil. Add tomato purée, wine, herbs, and seasoning and bring to a boil. Sprinkle on the flour and stir. Simmer for about 1 hour until all the vegetables are soft and most of the liquid has been taken up. Line a 25 × 35 cm (10 × 14 in) Swiss roll pan with greaseproof paper. Oil the paper well. Make a thick roux with the butter, flour, and milk. Separate eggs and add the yolks and seasoning to the roux. Next whip the egg whites until really stiff. Carefully fold into the sauce and pour into the lined pan. Cook at 200°C/400°F for 15 minutes. Remove from oven and pour two-thirds of the ratatouille mixture over the roulade. Roll up, removing the greaseproof paper as you go. Serve with remaining ratatouille on either side.

Roulade
5 eggs
12½ g (½ oz) butter
12½ g (½ oz) flour
125 ml (¼ pint) milk
salt and pepper

Ratatouille Filling
225 g (8 oz) onions
225 g (8 oz) zucchini
225 g (8 oz) tomatoes
1 aubergine
1 green pepper
2 tablespoons tomato
  purée
125 ml (¼ pint) white
  wine
½ tablespoon flour
½ teaspoon oregano
salt and pepper
cooking oil

Apple, Date, and Oatmeal Pie

Rub margarine into oats and flour. When crumbly mix with sugar and bind with a little water. Divide in two and press half into a 20 cm (8 in) flan pan. Fill with cooking apples that have been stewed with a little lemon rind and juice. Arrange dates on the top. Roll out the second half of the pastry and place on top of the pie. The pastry is very crumbly and it may be necessary to do this in two halves, joining the pastry with a little water across the center. Bake for 1 hour at 200°C/400° F. Serve hot or cold with fresh cream.

Pastry
100 g (4 oz) margarine
100 g (4 oz) porridge oats
100 g (4 oz) plain flour
100 g (4 oz) soft brown
  sugar
water to mix

Filling
480 g (1 lb) cooking
  apples
1 lemon
50 g (2 oz) stoned dates

Artichokes with Roquefort Dressing
Asparagus Delight with Baked Vegetable Rice
and Lettuce with Minted Peas
Plum Cheesecake

Artichokes with Roquefort Dressing

Beat oil and vinegar together with a fork and add sugar and seasoning. Finely chop gherkin, red pepper, and cheese and add to the dressing. Boil artichokes for 45 minutes in salted water with a dash of lemon juice. The artichokes are cooked when the leaves come away easily. Remove the center leaves and the choke and fill with dressing. The artichokes can be served this way hot or cold.

4 artichokes
lemon juice
salt

Dressing
120 ml (8 tablespoons) salad oil
60 ml (4 tablespoons) vinegar
6 small gherkins
¼ red pepper
75 g (3 oz) Roquefort cheese
salt and pepper
¼ teaspoon sugar

Asparagus Delight

Mix flour, salt, egg yolks, and milk. Whip egg white until really stiff and fold into the flour mixture. Use the batter to make 4 thick pancakes and keep warm. Finely chop mushrooms and fry in a little cooking oil. Make a roux sauce with the flour, butter, and the liquid from the can of asparagus made up to about 500 ml (1 pint) with milk. Add a little wine, season to taste. The sauce should be fairly thick. Divide in two and add the mushrooms to one half and the chopped asparagus to the other half. Lay one pancake on a serving dish and cover with half the mushroom sauce. Add another pancake and cover with half the asparagus sauce. Continue with alternate layers, ending with asparagus. Decorate with parsley and serve at once. Cut like a cake.

Pancakes
100 g (4 oz) flour
250 ml (½ pint) milk
2 eggs
salt

Fillings
40 g (1½ oz) flour
40 g (1½ oz) butter
milk
125 ml (¼ pint) wine
225 g (8 oz) mushrooms
350 g (12 oz) can
  asparagus
cooking oil
salt and pepper

Baked Vegetable Rice

Mix all ingredients and place in a casserole dish. Dot with butter and bake at 180°C/350°F for 1 hour.

50 g (2 oz) cooked rice
100 g (4 oz) cooked diced
  new potatoes
225 g (8 oz) diced
  vegetables
50 g (2 oz) diced red
  pepper
25 g (1 oz) grated cheese
butter
salt and pepper

Lettuce with Minted Peas

Wash lettuces and slice into 4 quarters. Melt butter in a pan and turn down the heat as low as possible. Add quartered lettuces and peas. Sprinkle with chopped mint and seasoning. Cover with a lid and simmer for about 8 minutes.

For a change, substitute finely chopped fried onion or ¼ teaspoon thyme for the mint.

hearts of 3 lettuces
700 g (1½ lb) thawed or fresh peas
6 teaspoons chopped fresh mint
150 g (3 oz) butter
salt and pepper

Plum Cheesecake*

Make the base by melting the margarine and adding the crushed biscuits. Press into the base of a 22.5 cm (9 in) loose-bottomed cake pan. Stone the plums and place on top of the base. Cream margarine and honey until light and fluffy and gradually beat in the cream cheese, sour cream, and egg yolks. Add a little lemon juice and some grated lemon rind. Whisk the egg whites until stiff and fold into the cream cheese mixture. Pour into the cake pan and bake for 1 hour at 180°C/350°F until set and turning golden brown. Reduce the oven to 150°C/300°F. Beat together yogurt and honey with a little more lemon juice and pour over the top of the cheesecake. Smooth with a palate knife. Bake for a further 15 minutes until set.

Base
25 g (1 oz) margarine or butter
9 digestive biscuits (see recipe for Coffee Cheesecake Mousse in Chapter 6)
225 g (8 oz) fresh, stewed or canned plums

Topping
50 g (2 oz) margarine
2 tablespoons runny honey
225 g (8 oz) Philadelphia cream cheese
125 ml (¼ pint) sour cream
2 eggs
1 lemon

Finish
125 ml (¼ pint) natural yogurt
1 tablespoon honey

*See Plate 4.

Cauliflower Soufflé
Potato and Mushroom Céleste
with Green Salad in Tarragon Dressing
Apricots Monte Carlo with Apricot Ice Cream

Cauliflower Soufflé

Steam cauliflower until soft and rub through a sieve or mouli. Leave to cool. Separate eggs and mix yolks with cauliflower and salt and pepper. Whip egg whites until stiff and fold into the cauliflower mixture. Pour into four individual soufflé dishes and bake at 200°C/400°F for 10–15 minutes until set and slightly brown on top.

1 cauliflower
3 eggs
salt and pepper

Potato and Mushroom Céleste

Peel and slice onions, potatoes, and tomatoes. Slice mushrooms and cheese and layer all ingredients in a casserole dish. Sprinkle the layers with herbs and seasoning. Finish off with a layer of potatoes and pour the cream over the top. Cover and bake at 200°C/400°F for about ¾ hour.

700 g (1½ lb) potatoes
3 onions
4 tomatoes
225 g (8 oz) mushrooms
225 g (8 oz) Brie cheese
1 teaspoon summer
  savory
½ teaspoon garlic salt
125 ml (¼ pint) heavy
  cream
salt and pepper

Green Salad in Tarragon Dressing

Wash lettuce and watercress and arrange in a bowl. Add sliced cucumber and green pepper. Mix dressing and pour over the salad.

Salad
1 lettuce
5 cm (2 in) cucumber
¼ green pepper
¼ bunch watercress

Dressing
60 ml (4 tablespoons) salad oil
30 ml (2 tablespoons) tarragon vinegar
¼ teaspoon sugar
1 teaspoon chopped fresh tarragon
salt and pepper

Apricots Monte Carlo

Put 1 scoop of honey ice cream into each of 4 glass dishes and leave in the refrigerator. Drain the apricots well. Melt the butter in a flambé dish or frying pan and add the apricots. Thoroughly warm through. Sprinkle over the pine kernels and pour over the Cognac. Heat gently and set light to the Cognac. Add a little of the apricot mixture to each dish, top with apricot ice cream, and serve decorated with the almonds, cherries, and walnuts.

4 scoops honey ice cream (see page 142)
4 scoops apricot ice cream (see below)
large can apricots
25 g (1 oz) butter
50 g (2 oz) pine kernels
3 liqueur glasses Cognac
12½ g (½ oz) almonds
12 red and green glacé cherries
4 walnuts

Apricot Ice Cream

Make purée by soaking 100 g (4 oz) apricots overnight, draining, and simmering with 150 ml (6 fl. oz) water. Rub through sieve or mouli, mix in the sugar, and allow to cool. Whip cream until stiff and fold in the fruit mixture. Spoon into a container, cover, and freeze.

250 ml (½ pint) heavy cream
100 g (4 oz) dried apricots
2 tablespoons Barbados sugar or honey
water

Egg and Tarragon Mousse
French Onion Tart
with Stuffed Potatoes and Savoy Peas
Orange Nut Crumble

Egg and Tarragon Mousse

Whip cream until fairly stiff. Sieve eggs, reserving 4 slices for garnish, and mix with cream. Prepare gelatine or gelozone as suggested in Chapter 4 and add to egg and cream mixture. Add remaining ingredients and mix well. Pour into individual dishes. Place a slice of egg on top of each and push into the mixture until it lies flat. Place in the refrigerator for at least 2 hours before serving. Garnish with a little more freshly chopped or dried tarragon. Serve with hot toast.

4 hard-boiled eggs
125 ml (¼ pint) heavy cream
45 ml (3 tablespoons) natural yogurt
1 teaspoon tarragon
¼ teaspoon Worcestershire sauce
12½ g (½ oz) gelatine or 2 teaspoons gelozone
60 ml (4 tablespoons) water
salt and pepper

French Onion Tart

Make pastry by rubbing fat into flour and salt and binding with egg yolk and a little water if necessary. Allow to rest and then roll out to line a 20 cm (8 in) flan pan. Gently fry sliced onions in cooking oil and add sugar. When the onions turn golden in color, drain off any excess fat and mix in beaten eggs, cream, cheese, and nutmeg. Season and spoon into the pastry case. Bake at 220°C/425°F for 40–45 minutes.

Pastry
75 g (3 oz) plain flour
25 g (1 oz) butter
1 egg yolk
salt

Filling
1¼ kg (2½ lb) onions
2 eggs
125 ml (¼ pint) heavy cream
50 g (2 oz) grated Gruyère cheese
1 teaspoon sugar
nutmeg
salt and pepper
cooking oil

133

Stuffed Potatoes

Scrub potatoes well and cut the skin all the way around each potato to prevent bursting in the oven. Bake in a hot oven 220°C/425°F for 45 minutes–1 hour depending on size. Meanwhile skin tomato and chop finely. Fry with finely chopped green pepper in a little butter. When the pepper is soft, allow mixture to cool. Mix into a paste with remaining butter and season to taste. When the potatoes are cooked, slit down the center and again at right angles to the first cut, and stuff each potato with a quarter of the pepper mixture.

4 potatoes
50 g (2 oz) butter
½ green pepper
1 tomato
salt and pepper

Savoy Peas

Wash and slice leeks and arrange in a casserole dish with the peas. Add crushed garlic, seasoning, and enough vegetable stock to come about one-third of the way up the vegetables. Bake on the lower shelf of the oven at 220°C/425°F for about 45 minutes.

225 g (8 oz) frozen or
　fresh peas
2 leeks
1 clove garlic
salt and pepper
vegetable stock

Orange Nut Crumble

Gently stew fruit until soft and place in the base of greased pie plate. Rub fat into flour and nuts until crumbly. Add sugar and grated orange rind. Pour the juice of the orange over the fruit and then sprinkle the crumble over the top. Press down lightly. Bake in a moderate oven 190°C/375°F for about ½ hour. Serve with fresh cream.

Note: This dish can be started at 220°C/425°F and then turned down after about 10–15 minutes.

450 g (1 lb) fruit (apples,
　plums, or gooseberries)
50 g (2 oz) Barbados
　sugar or honey
a little water

Crumble Topping
75 g (3 oz) butter or
　margarine
100 g (4 oz) plain flour
75 g (3 oz) Barbados
　sugar
50 g (2 oz) ground nuts
　(almonds, peanuts, or
　hazelnuts)
1 orange

Tomatoes Monte Carlo
Hot Cauliflower Mousse
with Haricots Verts and Orange Beetroot
Potted Cheese with Oatmeal Biscuits

Tomatoes Monte Carlo

Slice off the tops of the tomatoes and put on one side. Scoop out the centers of the tomatoes and the seeds. Chop and mix with remaining ingredients, adding sufficient cream or yogurt to moisten the mixture. Pile back into the tomatoes and cap with the sliced-off tops. Bake at 200°C/400°F for 20 minutes.

Note: Leftover risotto makes an excellent stuffing for baked tomatoes.

4 large Mediterranean
  tomatoes
75 g (3 oz) cooked rice
25 g (1 oz) cooked peas
a little sour cream or
  yogurt
½ teaspoon rosemary
salt and pepper

Hot Cauliflower Mousse

Steam cauliflower and retain liquid to include in vegetable stock. Rub cauliflower through sieve or mouli. Make a thick roux sauce with the butter, flour, and liquids. Add cinnamon and seasoning. Remove from heat and add beaten eggs and cauliflower. Pour into a greased soufflé dish, place dish in pan containing water enough to cover pan bottom, and bake 200°C/400°F for 1 hour.

1 large cauliflower
2 eggs
25 g (1 oz) butter
25 g (1 oz) flour
50 ml (2 fl.oz) white wine
  or dry sherry
150 ml (6 fl.oz) vegetable
  stock
150 ml (6 fl.oz) milk
cinnamon
salt and pepper

Orange Beetroot

Dice beetroot and heat through in a little butter. Add grated orange rind and orange juice. Heat through again, but do not boil. Sprinkle with sugar and black pepper and serve at once.

450 g (1 lb) cooked beetroot
15 ml (1 tablespoon) orange juice
rind of half an orange
butter
1 teaspoon sugar
black pepper

Potted Cheese

Grate cheese and mix with all other ingredients. Press into a small pot and leave in refrigerator for 3–4 days before serving with oatmeal biscuits (see below). Serve at room temperature.

225 g (8 oz) Cheddar cheese
30 ml (2 tablespoons) port
½ teaspoon mixed herbs
¼ teaspoon nutmeg
¼ teaspoon English mustard

Oatmeal Biscuits

Sift the flour and salt into a bowl and rub in the fat. Add oatmeal and sugar and mix to a firm dough with beaten egg. Turn onto a floured board and roll out thinly. Cut into 10 cm (4 in) rounds and place on a greased baking tray. Bake at 170°C/325°F for about 15–20 minutes until pale brown and crisp. Cool on a wire tray.

100 g (4 oz) plain flour
100 g (4 oz) fine oatmeal
1 level teaspoon salt
50 g (2 oz) white vegetable fat
25 g (1 oz) sugar
beaten egg

menu

Parmesan Eggs
Stuffed Avocados in Tomato Sauce
with Cauliflower Almandine, Duchesse Potatoes,
and Minted Peas
Caribbean Ice Cream

Parmesan Eggs

Mix French mustard with a little milk and gradually add remaining milk. Beat in eggs with a fork and add marjoram, Parmesan, and seasoning. Pour into individual baking dishes and place in a baking pan filled with 2 inches of water. Bake at 200°C/400°F for ¾ hour.

250 ml (½ pint) milk
4 eggs
1 teaspoon French
mustard
½ teaspoon marjoram
2 tablespoons Parmesan
cheese
salt and pepper

Stuffed Avocados in Tomato Sauce*

Peel and chop tomatoes and place in a pan with water, tomato paste, and seasoning. Bring to boil and simmer for 15–20 minutes. Blend and keep on one side. Mix cream cheese with herbs and plenty of salt and pepper. Peel, halve, and stone avocados and stuff the centers with cream cheese. Put halves back together and fix with a toothpick. Place in a casserole dish and cover with tomato sauce. Replace the lid and bake at 200°C/400°F for 20–30 minutes.

4 small avocados
100 g (4 oz) cream cheese
1 teaspoon basil
salt and pepper

Sauce
450 g (1 lb) tomatoes
2 tablespoons tomato
paste
350 ml (12 fl.oz) water
salt and pepper

Cauliflower Almandine**

Steam cauliflower until cooked and turn into a serving dish with the florets upward. Make a thin roux sauce with the butter, flour, and milk. Season and add almonds, retaining a few on one side. Pour over the cauliflower and sprinkle with toasted bread crumbs and remaining flaked almonds.

1 cauliflower
12½ g (½ oz) butter
12½ g (½ oz) flour
200 ml (8 fl.oz) milk
25 g (1 oz) flaked
almonds
25 g (1 oz) toasted bread
crumbs
salt and pepper

*See Plate 5 (middle).
**See Plate 5 (left).

Duchesse Potatoes*

Boil and mash potatoes and mix with butter and beaten eggs, retaining some of the egg to finish off the potatoes. Place potato mixture into an icing or decorating-type bag with a large nozzle and pipe into swirls on a greased baking sheet. Bake at 200°C/400°F until lightly browned (about 20–30 minutes). Brush the tops with the remaining egg when half done.

450 g (1 lb) potatoes
2 eggs
25 g (1 oz) butter

Caribbean Ice Cream

Halve pineapples and scoop out the flesh, leaving the skins intact. Refrigerate skins in a plastic bag. Purée pineapple with rum and mix with sugar. Whip cream and fold in the fruit mixture. Spoon into a container and freeze. Serve in the pineapple skins decorated with cherries and flaked almonds.

2 small pineapples
250 ml (½ pint) heavy cream
15 ml (1 tablespoon) dark rum
2 tablespoons Barbados sugar
glacé cherries
flaked almonds

menu

Green Beans with Peanut Dressing
Cottage Cheese Pancakes with Avocado Sauce,
Buttered Vegetable Medley, and Boiled Potatoes
Pineapple and Ginger Crush

Green Beans with Peanut Dressing

Cook French beans, drain, and allow to cool. Mix peanut butter, yogurt, and milk and add oregano. Place beans in individual dishes and pour the dressing over the top.

450 g (1 lb) French beans
2 teaspoons peanut butter
15 ml (1 tablespoon) milk
22 ml (1½ tablespoons) yogurt
½ teaspoon oregano

*See Plate 5 (right).

Cottage Cheese Pancakes with Avocado Sauce

Beat egg with a little milk and pour over sieved flour and salt. Mix to a stiff batter and beat well. Add remaining milk and leave to stand for 1 hour. Make 8 pancakes with the mixture and spread each with seasoned cottage cheese. Roll up and place in the base of an ovenproof dish. Make a roux sauce with the butter, flour, and milk. Peel and stone avocados and sieve into sauce. Season to taste and pour over the pancakes. Place in a moderate oven 180°C/350°F for ½ hour. Serve garnished with sprigs of watercress.

Pancakes
100 g (4 oz) flour
250 ml (½ pint) milk
1 egg
salt

Filling
450 g (1 lb) cottage cheese
salt and pepper

Sauce
50 g (2 oz) butter
50 g (2 oz) flour
500 ml (1 pint) milk
3 ripe avocados
salt and pepper

Garnish
sprigs of watercress

Buttered Vegetable Medley

Cook diced carrots or baby onions in boiling water for 10 minutes. Add remaining vegetables and cook for a further 5 minutes. Drain and add butter before serving.

100 g (4 oz) frozen or
  fresh peas
100 g (4 oz) frozen or
  canned sweet corn
100 g (4 oz) cut green
  beans
100 g (4 oz) diced carrots
  or baby onions
25 g (1 oz) butter

Pineapple and Ginger Crush

Finely chop stem ginger and mix with pineapple and yogurt. Chill before serving.

325 g (12 oz) crushed or
  chopped pineapple
1 small carton, 150 ml (6
  fl.oz), plain yogurt
1–2 pieces stem ginger
  according to taste

Savory Stuffed Apples
Spinach Lasagne with Tomato Sauce,
Green Beans, and Baked Fennel
Honey Ice Cream Cassata

Savory Stuffed Apples

Wash, halve, and core apples. Slice each apple half into 2 layers. Finely chop onion and mix with all other ingredients. Place 4 slices of apple in the base of an ovenproof dish. Cover with half the stuffing. Place another layer of apple on top and finish off with the remaining stuffing. Bake uncovered in a fairly hot oven 200°C/400°F for 1 hour.

2 large cooking apples
50 g (2 oz) brown bread
  crumbs
25 g (1 oz) ground
  peanuts
1 small onion
2 teaspoons toasted
ground sesame seeds
2 teaspoons tomato purée
½ teaspoon oregano
125 ml (¼ pint) tomato
  juice
salt and pepper

Spinach Lasagne with Tomato Sauce

Cook lasagne in boiling salted water and drain. Wash spinach and place in pan with a little butter. Cook gently until the spinach is soft. Spread each slice of lasagne with cottage cheese, spinach, and celery seed. Roll up and place in a casserole dish. Make tomato sauce by frying finely chopped onions. Add chopped tomatoes, tomato purée, oregano, and seasoning. Simmer until the vegetables are cooked through. Purée and pour over the lasagne. Sprinkle with a little Parmesan and bake 200°C/400°F for about 15 minutes.

8 pieces lasagne

Filling
350 g (12 oz) cottage cheese
1 kg (2 lb 2 oz) spinach
1 knob butter
1 teaspoon celery seed or celery salt

Sauce
450 g (1 lb) tomatoes
1 onion
2 tablespoons tomato purée
1 teaspoon oregano
salt and pepper
Parmesan cheese

Baked Fennel

Wash and roughly slice fennel. Place in a casserole dish and sprinkle with finely chopped shallots or spring onions. Mix Marmite with warm stock and pour over the top of the vegetables. Season to taste. Cover and bake in a fairly hot oven 200°C/400°F for about 1 hour.

2 large heads of fennel
3 or 4 shallots or spring onions
60 ml (4 tablespoons) vegetable stock
1/2 teaspoon Marmite or yeast extract
salt and pepper

Honey Ice Cream Cassata

Make ice cream by whisking eggs and honey until thick and pale in color. Next whip cream and milk until really stiff. Quickly fold into the egg mixture and pour into a container and freeze. When the ice cream is frozen, spoon a third into a small chilled metal mold and press down. Spread the remaining two-thirds around the edge of the mold, leaving a well in the center. Whip cream and icing sugar to make the filling and fold in the chopped fruit and almonds. Spoon into the well in the center of the ice cream, cover with plastic wrap, and return to freezer. Just before serving, turn on to a serving dish and keep in the refrigerator until ready to place on the table.

Ice Cream
2 eggs
1 dessertspoon runny honey
75 ml (3 fl.oz) heavy cream
50 ml (2 fl.oz) milk

Filling
125 ml (¼ pint) heavy cream
1 tablespoon icing sugar
25 g (1 oz) glacé peel
25 g (1 oz) raisins
25 g (1 oz) glacé cherries
25 g (1 oz) flaked almonds

menu

Stilton Pâté
Green Pepper and Hazelnut Bake
with Tomato Sauce, Braised Endive,
and Parsley Buttered Potatoes
Lime and Ginger Syllabub

Stilton Pâté

Make a thick roux sauce with the butter, flour, and milk. Cool thoroughly and add all other ingredients including finely chopped olives. Spoon into individual dishes and serve chilled with fingers of hot toast.

100 g (4 oz) grated Stilton cheese
5 ml (1 teaspoon) mayonnaise
25 g (1 oz) butter
25 g (1 oz) flour
200 ml (8 fl.oz) milk
1 clove garlic
salt and pepper
4 stuffed olives

Green Pepper and Hazelnut Bake

Grate onions and green peppers and finely chop mushrooms. Mix all ingredients together and moisten with the puréed contents of the can of tomatoes. The mixture should be very moist. Shape into an oblong and roll in flaked oats or millet. Place on a greased baking pan and flatten slightly. Bake at 200°C/400°F for ¾ hour. Serve with tomato sauce.

2 large onions
2 small green peppers
100 g (4 oz) mushrooms
100 g (4 oz) ground hazelnuts
100 g (4 oz) bread crumbs
2 tablespoons soya flour
¼ teaspoon celery seed or celery salt
¼ teaspoon garlic salt
1 teaspoon fresh or dried mixed herbs
½ teaspoon summer savory
425 g (15 oz) can tomatoes
oat or millet flakes

Braised Endive

Wash endive and place in a casserole dish. Fry onion until well browned in a little oil and add stock, Marmite, and seasoning. Pour over the endive. Cover and bake at 200°C/400°F for ½ hour.

4 endive
1 small onion
¼ teaspoon Marmite or yeast extract
125 ml (¼ pint) vegetable stock
salt and pepper
cooking oil

Lime
and Ginger Syllabub

Dissolve honey in ginger wine. Add lime cordial and cream and whip until thick. Chill and serve topped with crushed ginger cookies.

250 ml (½ pint) heavy
  cream
45 ml (3 tablespoons)
  ginger wine
15 ml (1 tablespoon) lime
  cordial
1 tablespoon runny
  honey
4–6 ginger cookies

menu

Fennel and Avocado Salad
African Curried Vegetables with Dahl,
Banana Sambal, and Pilao Rice
Normandy Apple Tart

Fennel
and Avocado Salad

Parboil fennel for about 5 minutes. Drain and slice. Finely slice red pepper and tomatoes and mix with fennel. Add herbs and dressing. Just before serving, peel and slice avocado and mix in.

2 fennel heads
1 avocado
1 red pepper
2 tomatoes
½ teaspoon mixed herbs
60 ml (4 tablespoons)
  vinaigrette dressing

African Curried Vegetables

Fry onion in oil with spices until lightly browned. Add chopped vegetables and water. Bring to boil and simmer for about 30–40 minutes. Drain liquid and mix with peanut butter. Return to pan and correct seasoning. Simmer for a further 5–10 minutes before serving.

1 onion
500 ml (1 pint) water
1 teaspoon curry powder
1 teaspoon cumin
1 teaspoon coriander
¼ teaspoon ground ginger
2 cloves
4 cardamoms
1 heaping tablespoon peanut butter
cooking oil
450 g (1 lb) mixed vegetables: cauliflower, carrots, and potatoes
salt and pepper

Dahl

Place lentils in a pan with water and bring to boil. Simmer for ¾ hour. Add turmeric and salt and continue cooking until lentils are really soft (about another 30 minutes). Fry sliced onion, garlic, and ginger until lightly browned and add to the dahl just before serving.

100 g (4 oz) lentils
500 ml (1 pint) water
½ teaspoon turmeric
salt
1 small onion
1 clove garlic (optional)
1 piece stem ginger

Banana Sambal

Cook unpeeled banana in boiling water until soft. Remove from water and allow to cool. Peel, mash, and mix with finely chopped onion and chili. Add vinegar, yogurt, and seasoning. Mix well.

1 banana
½ small onion
1 green chili without seeds
10 ml (2 teaspoons) cider vinegar
½ small carton natural yogurt
salt and pepper

Pilao Rice

Fry onion in butter and add rice and spices. Continue cooking for 5 minutes. Add yogurt and water. Bring to boil and simmer until all liquid is taken up (about 30–40 minutes). Correct seasoning and pile into a serving dish and if necessary dry off in a warm oven.

150 g (6 oz) rice
1 onion
25 g (1 oz) butter
3 peppercorns
1 cardamom
1 clove
½ small carton yogurt
750 ml (1½ pints) water
salt

Normandy Apple Tart

Make pastry by rubbing fat into sugar and flour until the mixture resembles fine bread crumbs. Bind with about half a beaten egg. Press into a 20 cm (8 in) flan pan. Peel and slice cooking apples and simmer with a very little water until soft. Allow to cool and spoon into the pastry case. Peel and slice eating apples and arrange on top of the apple purée. Brush with apricot jam. Bake at 220°C/425°F for about 45 minutes until the apples begin to brown.

Pastry
100 g (4 oz) plain flour
50 g (2 oz) butter
50 g (2 oz) sugar
beaten egg

Filling
450 g (1 lb) cooking
   apples
3 eating apples
apricot jam

menu

Grape and Celery Salad
Courgette and Dill Soup
Avocado Risotto with Mexican Sauce
and Red and Green Pepper Salad*
Hazelnut Soufflé

*See page 84.

Grape and Celery Salad

Halve and deseed the grapes. Finely dice the celery, green pepper, and cucumber and add to grapes. Mix all ingredients together with yogurt and serve slightly chilled.

225 g (8 oz) white grapes
7.5 cm (3 in) cucumber
4 sticks celery
¼ green pepper
30 ml (2 tablespoons) yogurt
¼ teaspoon rosemary

Courgette (Zucchini) and Dill Soup

Melt butter in pan and add chopped onions. Sauté until transparent. Add sugar and sherry and bring to boil. Add coarsely chopped zucchini, dill seed, vegetable stock, and seasoning. Bring to boil and simmer for 45 minutes. Rub through sieve or mouli. Correct seasoning and reheat. Serve with a tablespoon of cream in each bowl.

450 g (1 lb) zucchini
1 medium onion
25 g (1 oz) butter
75 ml (3 fl.oz) cooking sherry
625 ml (1¼ pints) vegetable stock
1 teaspoon dill seed
½ teaspoon sugar
salt and pepper
60 ml (4 tablespoons) double cream

Avocado Risotto

Finely chop onion and fry in butter until transparent. Add rice and continue frying gently for 3–4 minutes. Add wine and bring to boil. Continue cooking until all the wine is absorbed, stirring from time to time. Add herbs, seasoning, chopped avocado, and vegetable stock. Continue cooking until the rice has absorbed all the stock (about 20–30 minutes). Add more stock if the rice shows signs of drying out too much.

350 g (12 oz) rice
2 avocados
1 large onion
50 g (2 oz) raisins
250 ml (½ pint) white wine
500 ml (1 pint) vegetable stock
50 g (2 oz) butter
½ teaspoon mixed herbs
salt and pepper

Mexican Sauce

Finely chop peppers and garlic and fry in cooking oil for 5 minutes. Add chopped tomatoes and all other ingredients and bring to boil. Simmer for 20 minutes. Liquidize and correct seasoning. Reheat and serve with risotto.

1 red pepper
1 green pepper
8 tomatoes
1 clove garlic
1 teaspoon coriander
2 cloves
½ teaspoon chili powder
250 ml (½ pint) vegetable
　stock or water
cooking oil
salt and pepper

Hazelnut Soufflé

Roast hazelnuts on an ungreased baking sheet for 15 minutes at 200°C/400°F. Remove from the oven and roll on a dry working surface so that the brown skin comes off. Grind the nuts finely. Heat the milk, butter, salt, and sugar in a pan. Slowly add the flour. Stir until the mixture forms a smooth paste that comes away easily from the sides of the pan. Leave to cool. Beat together the egg yolks and grated hazelnuts and add to the sauce mixture. Whisk the egg whites until they form stiff peaks and fold into the mixture. Grease a soufflé dish and fill with the mixture. Place on the middle shelf of a preheated oven and bake at 180°C/350°F for 1 hour. Serve at once.

100 g (4 oz) shelled
　hazelnuts
125 ml (¼ pint) milk
25 g (1 oz) butter
pinch of salt
50 g (2 oz) sugar
60 g (2½ oz) plain flour
4 eggs, separated
butter to grease soufflé
　dish

menu

Hungarian Apple Soup
Cheese Fondue and Salads
Citrus Melon

Hungarian Apple Soup

Gently fry chopped onions, garlic, eating apples, red pepper, and gherkins in cooking oil. After 3–4 minutes add stock, seasoning, and chives. Bring to a boil and simmer for 20 minutes. Stir in sour cream and serve sprinkled with more chives. For a slightly thicker soup, add fresh bread crumbs.

4 eating apples
2 onions
1 red pepper
2 large gherkins or 1 pickled cucumber
1 clove garlic
500 ml (1 pint) vegetable stock
½ teaspoon sugar
½ teaspoon paprika
1 tablespoon chopped chives
100 ml (4 fl.oz) sour cream
50 g (2 oz) bread crumbs (optional)
cooking oil

Cheese Fondue

Peel the garlic clove. Score one edge and rub over the fondue dish. Put in the water, butter, salt, pepper, and nutmeg and bring a boil. Dice the cheese and add to the water. Leave for about 15 minutes to melt. If the mixture seems too thick, add 1 tablespoon of water at a time until consistency is right. Slice the bread. Light the fondue burner to keep the mixture warm but not boiling. Each guest spears a piece of bread on a fondue fork and dips into the fondue. Serve with a medley of salads from Chapter 6.

600 g (1 lb 6 oz) Emmental cheese
1 clove garlic
grated nutmeg
125 ml (¼ pint) hot water
25 g (1 oz) butter
salt and pepper
1 French bread

Citrus Melon

Roast peanuts in the oven at 180°C/350°F for about 20 minutes. Halve the melon. Scoop out the seeds and flesh. Discard seeds and chop flesh. Mix with segmented and chopped grapefruit and oranges. Pile back into the two melon shells. Chop peanuts and mix with sugar and cinnamon and sprinkle over the fruit.

1 small honeydew melon
1 grapefruit
2 oranges
50 g (2 oz) peanuts
25 g (1 oz) sugar
¼ teaspoon cinnamon

Gala Buffets **11**

Recipes in this chapter are for 12 people.

Love Apples
Hot Cauliflower Terrine
with Spanish Lentils, Savoy Gratin,
and Chinese Cabbage with Juniper Berries
Lemon Tart

Love Apples

Peel and slice tomatoes. Place in individual baking dishes and cover with sherry and season. Place in a moderate oven 190°C/375°F for 20 minutes. Sprinkle with grated cheese and cream and continue cooking for 4–5 minutes. Serve at once.

12 good-sized tomatoes
125 ml (¼ pint) heavy
 cream
50 g (2 oz) grated cheese
sherry
salt and pepper

150

Hot Cauliflower Terrine

Remove outer leaves and excess stalk from cauliflower and steam until tender. Drain and mash to a purée. Finely chop the onion and fry in butter until soft. Mix mashed cauliflower with onions, bread crumbs, nutmeg, salt and pepper, sour cream, and beaten eggs. Grease a large casserole or soufflé dish and spoon in the cauliflower mixture. Bake at 190°C/375°F for 1 hour. Sprinkle the top with chopped parsley and serve at once.

2 cauliflowers
2 onions
150 g (6 oz) fresh bread crumbs
250 ml (1½ pints) sour cream
4 eggs
nutmeg
salt and pepper
fresh parsley
butter

Spanish Lentils

Wash lentils and simmer with Marmite and water for ½ hour. Add finely chopped vegetables, seasoning, and marjoram. Continue to simmer for about 1 hour until all the vegetables are cooked and the mixture is fairly thick.

350 g (12 oz) lentils
1½ liters (3 pints) water
2 teaspoons Marmite or yeast extract
225 g (8 oz) onions
225 g (8 oz) tomatoes
½ green pepper
2 teaspoons marjoram
salt and pepper

Savoy Gratin

Peel potatoes and simmer in milk until half cooked. Transfer to open gratin dish, retaining just enough milk to come halfway up the potatoes. Pour over cream and sprinkle with salt, pepper, nutmeg, and Gruyère. Bake at 190°C/375°F for ½ hour.

1½ kg (3 lb) potatoes
50 g (2 oz) Gruyère cheese
250 ml (¼ pint) fresh cream
milk
salt and pepper
nutmeg

Chinese Cabbage with Juniper Berries

Wash cabbage and coarsely chop. Simmer with juniper berries in a very little water for 15 minutes. Drain and serve with plenty of black pepper.

900 g (2 lb) Chinese cabbage
1 teaspoon juniper berries
black pepper
water

Lemon Tart

Pastry
225 g (8 oz) plain flour
100 g (4 oz) butter
100 g (4 oz) sugar
1 egg

Make pastry by rubbing butter into flour and sugar until it resembles fine bread crumbs. Bind with an egg. This makes very crumbly pastry. Press into two 20 cm (8 in) flan pans. Melt butter. Remove from heat and add sugar. Whisk in eggs one by one and then add grated rind of 3–4 lemons and whisk in the juice of all of them. Pour into the pastry case and bake at 220°C/425°F for 40–45 minutes. Leave to cool.

Filling
100 g (4 oz) butter
325 g (12 oz) sugar
6 eggs
5–6 lemons

menu

Green Pea Soufflé
Glazed Vegetable Pâté and Scrambled Egg Flan with Pepper Slaw and Potato Salad*
Apricot Cheesecake

*See page 87, multiply quantities by three.

Green Pea Soufflé

Prepare gelatine or gelozone as directed in Chapter 4. Dissolve Marmite in water and add peas. Bring to boil and simmer for 5–8 minutes. Allow to cool and then blend. Whisk egg whites and cream separately. Add whipped cream and dissolved gelatine or gelozone to the pea purée and mix well. Next fold in the whipped egg whites. Pour into individual dishes and chill for 3–4 hours in the refrigerator. Serve with brown bread and butter.

700 g (1½ lb) frozen peas
3 egg whites
170 ml (7½ fl.oz) heavy cream
750 ml (1½ pints) water
1 teaspoon Marmite or yeast extract
18 g (¾ oz) gelatine or 3 teaspoons gelozone

Glazed Vegetable Pâté

Finely grate carrot and mince mushrooms, onions, bread crumbs, and cottage cheese. Grind soya beans. Mix all ingredients together. Spoon into a large foil-lined bread pan, place in pan containing water to cover the bottom, and bake at 190°C/375°F for 1 hour. Remove foil and allow to cool. Dissolve gelatine and mix with warm water and Marmite or sprinkle agar-agar over boiling water and Marmite. Place pâté on large serving dish and decorate with sliced gherkin and bay leaves. Pour over the glaze and place in the refrigerator to set.

225 g (8 oz) cooked soya beans
225 g (8 oz) mushrooms
2 medium onions
100 g (4 oz) bread crumbs
100 g (4 oz) cottage cheese
100 g (4 oz) ground peanuts
1 carrot
4 eggs
½ teaspoon fennel seed
1 teaspoon thyme
garlic salt
1 teaspoon celery seed or salt
black pepper
cooking oil

Glaze
2 teaspoons agar-agar or 12½ g (½ oz) gelatine
375 ml (¾ pint) water
1 teaspoon Marmite or yeast extract
gherkin and bay leaves to garnish

Scrambled Egg Flan

Make pastry by rubbing butter into flour and salt. Bind with a little water. Allow to rest and then roll out to line two 20 cm (8 in) flan pans. Bake at 200°C/400°F for 25–30 minutes without opening oven door during this time. Allow to cool. Scramble the beaten eggs with milk and butter and season to taste. Cook peas and peel and slice tomatoes. Allow all ingredients to cool. Spread scrambled eggs in flan cases and decorate with sliced tomatoes, peas, and mint.

Pastry
150 g (6 oz) plain flour
75 g (3 oz) butter
salt
30–45 ml (2–3
    tablespoons) water

Filling
12 eggs
25 g (1 oz) butter
125 ml (¼ pint) milk
salt and pepper

Garnish
225 g (8 oz) frozen peas
6 small tomatoes
sprigs of fresh mint

Pepper Slaw

Finely shred cabbage, peppers, and gherkins. Toss all ingredients in mayonnaise and add flaked almonds. Season to taste.

½ large white cabbage
2 green peppers
2 red peppers
4 gherkins
2 tablespoons flaked
    almonds
60 ml (4 tablespoons)
    mayonnaise
salt and pepper

Apricot Cheesecake

Crush digestive biscuits and mix with melted butter. Bake in a very low oven 150°C/300°F for 8 minutes. Allow to cool. Separate egg yolks and beat with cream cheese and sugar. Prepare gelatine or gelozone, as suggested in Chapter 4, and add to mixture. Whip cream and egg whites separately and fold first the cream and then the egg white into the cheese mixture. Pour on to cool base and leave to set. Top with cooked fresh or dried apricots and decorate with flaked almonds.

Base
1½ packages digestive biscuits (see recipe for Chocolate Cheesecake Mousse in Chapter 6)
150 g (6 oz) butter

Topping
700 g (1½ lb) Philadelphia cream cheese
3 eggs
225 g (8 oz) sugar
375 ml (¾ pint) heavy cream
36 g (1½ oz) gelatine or 6 teaspoons gelozone
1½ kg (3 lb) stewed fresh apricots or 700 g (1½ lb) dried apricots soaked and puréed
a little water
flaked almonds

menu

Cream of Chick Pea Soup
Mushroom Terrine and Asparagus Cheese
with Pickled Vegetables and Toast or French Bread
Strawberry Crunchy Cream

Cream of Chick Pea Soup

Soak chick peas overnight. Drain and place in a pan with stock. Bring to boil and simmer for 1½ hours until cooked. Rub through a mouli and return to heat. Add black pepper and egg yolks mixed with cream. Reheat, but do not boil. Serve with fried bread croûtons.

450 g (1 lb) chick peas
2 liters (4 pints) vegetable stock or water
black pepper
125 ml (¼ pint) heavy cream
2 egg yolks
fried bread croûtons

Mushroom Terrine

Finely chop onions and mushrooms and gently fry until soft. Mix with all other ingredients and spoon into a foil-lined bread pan or terrine dish. Place in water-covered pan and bake at 180°C/350°F for 1 hour.

700 g (1½ lb) mushrooms
100 g (4 oz) ground almonds
100 g (4 oz) ground cashew nuts
50 g (2 oz) bread crumbs
2 eggs
2 onions
1 teaspoon Worcestershire sauce
1 teaspoon garlic salt
2 teaspoons marjoram
2 teaspoons oregano
cooking oil
salt and pepper

Asparagus Cheese

Finely chop or purée asparagus. Melt butter and mix with asparagus and cream cheese. Season to taste and place in refrigerator to set. Serve with fingers of brown toast or French bread.

3 × 175 g (7 oz, dry weight) cans asparagus
350 g (12 oz) cream cheese
150 g (6 oz) butter
salt and pepper

Pickled Vegetables

Wash and slice chosen vegetables and parboil in salted water. Drain and simmer in pickling liquor until fully cooked. Allow to cool and serve partially drained.

900 g (2 lb) mixed vegetables: cauliflower, celery hearts, carrots, beans, leeks, aubergines, etc.

Pickling Liquor
250 ml (½ pint) water
250 ml (½ pint) cider vinegar
125 ml (¼ pint) olive oil
juice of 4 lemons
8 peppercorns
2 cloves
4 bay leaves
2 sprigs thyme
salt

Strawberry Crunchy Cream

Whisk egg white very stiffly and then gradually whisk in half the sugar. Fold in the rest of the sugar, nuts, bicarbonate of soda, and essence. Spread meringue about 1 cm (½ in) thick on rice paper on a baking tray. Bake in a low oven 130°C/250°F for abour 2½ hours until the meringue is crisp underneath. Leave till cold. Break into pieces. Whip cream until just thick. Halve strawberries and just before serving, mix cream, strawberries, and meringue pieces in a large bowl.

450 g (1 lb) strawberries
500 ml (1 pint) heavy cream
2 egg whites
100 g (4 oz) caster sugar
50 g (2 oz) ground walnuts
pinch bicarbonate of soda
vanilla essence

Colombian Onion Soup
Curried Bean Pie and Cardamom Cheese Pie
with Devonshire Carrots and Turnips
and Creole Potatoes
Cinnamon Apple Cake

Colombian Onion Soup

Peel and slice onions and cover with water and lemon juice. Leave for 1 hour and then drain well. Fry in butter for 10–15 minutes and add flour and seasoning. Stir well and add milk and stock. Bring to boil and simmer for 45 minutes. If the soup is too thick, add a little white wine and correct seasoning.

1½ kg (3 lb) onions
juice of 1 lemon
water
50 g (2 oz) butter
500 ml (1 pint) vegetable stock
750 ml (1½ pints) milk
2 tablespoons plain flour
white wine
salt and pepper

Curried Bean Pie

Soak beans overnight in water and drain. Fry finely chopped onion, garlic, carrots, and spices in cooking oil for 5 minutes. Add flour and stir well. Then add beans and water and bring to boil. Simmer till beans are soft and the mixture fairly thick. Allow to cool. Rub fat into flour and salt and mix with water to make the pastry. Roll out and line two 20 cm (8 in) pie plates. Fill with bean mixture and cover with pastry lids. Fork the edges and prick the centers and bake at 200°C/400°F for 45 minutes or until the pastry is cooked.

Pastry
225 g (8 oz) plain flour
100 g (4 oz) butter
salt water

Filling
450 g (1 lb) haricot beans
4 onions
2 carrots
4 cloves garlic
4 tablespoons plain flour
4 teaspoons cumin seed
2 teaspoons chili powder
1 teaspoon ginger
8 cardamoms
4 cloves
750 ml (1½ pints)
    vegetable stock or water
cooking oil
salt and pepper

Cardamom Cheese Pie

Rub fat into flour and salt and bind with water. Roll out and line two 20 cm (8 in) pie dishes. Chop hard-boiled eggs and mix with remaining filling ingredients and spoon into pastry bases. Cover with pastry lids. Fork the edges and prick the center. Bake at 200°C/400°F for 45 minutes or until the pastry is cooked.

Pastry
225 g (8 oz) plain flour
100 g (4 oz) butter
salt
water

Filling
350 g (12 oz) grated
    Cheddar cheese
225 g (8 oz) raisins
8 hard-boiled eggs
2 tablespoons sugar
2 crushed cardamom
    seeds

Devonshire Carrots and Turnips

Peel and coarsely chop carrots and turnips. Place in a casserole dish. Dissolve honey in cider and pour over the vegetables. Season and cover. Bake at 200°C/400°F for 1 hour.

700 g (1½ lb) carrots
700 g (1½ lb) turnips
125 ml (¼ pint) dry cider
1 tablespoon honey
salt and pepper

Creole Potatoes

Peel and slice potatoes and layer with butter, seasoning, and tomato paste in a casserole dish. Fill two-thirds of the dish with milk. Cover and bake at 200°C/400°F for 1 hour.

1½ kg (3 lb) potatoes
2 tablespoons tomato
    purée
25 g (1 oz) butter
milk
salt and pepper

Cinnamon Apple Cake

Sift the flour into a bowl. Make a hollow in the center and mix in the salt and water. Flake the fat and add to the mixture. Rub in quickly, working from the outside in, to make a smooth dough. Leave to stand in the refrigerator for 30 minutes.

Grease a loose-bottomed cake pan. Line with the rolled-out dough, working the dough up the sides of the pan. Fill with the apple purée. Peel and halve the apples. Core and slice. Place the slices on the purée in circles. Mix the jam with the apricot brandy and spread over the apples. Sprinkle over the almonds. Bake for 30 minutes at 200°C/400°F. Leave to cool and cut into 12 slices.

Base
200 g (7 oz) flour
150 g (6 oz) butter or margarine
30 ml (2 tablespoons) cold water
pinch of salt

Topping
450 g (1 lb) apple purée flavored with 1 teaspoon cinnamon
450 g (1 lb) apples
100 g (4 oz) apricot jam
45 ml (3 tablespoons) apricot brandy
67 g (2½ oz) split almonds

menu

Ratatouille
Blue Cheese Quiche and Leek and Sesame Flan with Summer Salad and Rice Cake
Chocolate Choux Ring

Ratatouille

Wash and slice zucchini and onions and dice the other vegetables. Fry onions in cooking oil for 5 minutes and add all other vegetables. Continue to fry gently for 10 minutes. Add remaining ingredients ending with the wine, stir well, and bring to boil. Simmer for 45 minutes, adding more wine if the mixture gets too thick. Leave to cool and serve in individual dishes topped with freshly chopped parsley.

450 g (1 lb) tomatoes
450 g (1 lb) zucchini
1 large aubergine
1 green pepper
1 red pepper
3 large onions
2 tablespoons tomato
 paste
1 tablespoon flour
2 teaspoons oregano
salt and black pepper
cooking oil
125 ml (¼ pint) white
 wine
chopped parsley

Blue Cheese Quiche

Make pastry by rubbing butter into flour and salt. Bind with water. Allow to rest and then roll out to line two 20 cm (8 in) flan pans. Grate Cheddar cheese and mix with beaten eggs, cream, and a little milk. Season and pour half the mixture into each flan. If the mixture is a little sparse, add a little more milk and fork in, taking care not to pierce the pastry. Place on tray and bake at 200°C/400°F for ½ hour. Top each flan with grated blue cheese and return to the oven for a further 20 minutes or until cooked through. Leave to cool.

Pastry
150 g (6 oz) plain flour
75 g (3 oz) butter
salt
30–45 ml (2–3
 tablespoons) water

Filling
6 eggs
150 g (6 oz) Cheddar
 cheese
100 g (4 oz) blue cheese
 (Danish Blue, Stilton, or
 Roquefort)
250 ml (½ pint) heavy
 cream
milk
salt and pepper

Leek and Sesame Flan

Make pastry by rubbing butter into flour and salt. Bind
with water. Allow to rest and then roll out to line two
20 cm (8 in) flan pans. Steam leeks in a very little water
till cooked. Drain well and leave to cool. Place in the
base of the flan pans and sprinkle with sesame seeds
and salt and pepper. Grate cheese and mix with beaten
eggs and cream. Pour over the leeks. If the flans need
to be a little fuller, add some milk and mix in with a
fork, taking care not to pierce the pastry. Bake at 200°C/
400°F for 1 hour or until the flan is golden all over the
top and the center is cooked through. Leave to cool.

Pastry
150 g (6 oz) plain flour
75 g (3 oz) butter
salt
30–45 ml (2–3
   tablespoons) water

Filling
700 g (1½ lb) leeks
150 g (6 oz) Cheddar
   cheese
6 eggs
250 ml (½ pint) heavy
   cream
milk
salt and pepper
1 teaspoon toasted
   ground sesame seeds

Summer Salad

Mix French mustard, sugar, and seasoning into oil and
vinegar. Mix all other ingredients together and pour
over the dressing.

450 g (1 lb) fresh new
   peas
450 g (1 lb) finely sliced
   new green beans
10 cm (4 in) cucumber,
   diced
1 diced green pepper
125 ml (¼ pint) oil and
   vinegar dressing
2 teaspoons French
   mustard
1 teaspoon sugar
salt and pepper

Rice Cake

Cook the rice in boiling salted water. Drain well and dry over a low heat or in the oven. Leave to cool. Grate the beetroot and mix with peanuts and chopped hard-boiled eggs. Then add the cream and stir well. Pack into a bread pan and weight the top. Chill well and serve garnished with watercress.

450 g (1 lb) rice
225 g (8 oz) cooked beetroot
250 ml (½ pint) sour cream
4 hard-boiled eggs
75 g (3 oz) roasted peanuts
salt and pepper
watercress

Chocolate Choux Ring

Place water, salt, and butter in a pan and bring to a boil. Add flour and beat well to a smooth paste that leaves the sides of the pan clean. Remove from heat and add egg yolks and vanilla. Beat well and add the remaining eggs one by one, beating all the time. Grease a baking pan and pipe 2 rings of choux pastry on it. Bake at 220°C/425°F until the choux ring is risen and crisp. Continue cooking until the centers are dry and the outside fairly brown. Place on a cooking tray and slit around the outside of the rings about halfway up. Leave to cool. Meanwhile make cocoa with boiling water, to the normal strength, and leave to cool. Whip cold cocoa with sugar and cream and use this mixture to fill the centers of the rings. Make the topping by breaking the chocolate into small pieces and placing in a bowl over warm water. Allow to dissolve. Add icing sugar and water and stir until well mixed and smooth. Spread over the top of each ring and serve when the icing is set.

Choux pastry
225 g (8 oz) plain flour
500 ml (1 pint) water
100 g (4 oz) butter
2 egg yolks
4 eggs
¼ teaspoon salt
1 teaspoon vanilla essence

Filling
500 ml (1 pint) cream
150 g (6 oz) sugar
200 ml (8 fl.oz) cocoa

Topping
225 g (8 oz) icing sugar
75 g (3 oz) plain chocolate
125 ml (¼ pint) water

Apple and Celery Soup
Mali Pie and Artichoke and Egg Flan,
Sprouts with Nutmeg, and Potatoes Provençale
Apricots in Ginger

Apple and Celery Soup

Melt butter in pan and fry chopped onion. Add sherry and bring to boil. Next add chopped apples and celery and water. Sprinkle with cumin and seasoning and bring to boil. Simmer for 45 minutes and pass through mouli. Add sour cream and reheat before serving. Do not boil. Serve garnished with small almond cookies.

25 g (1 oz) butter
3 onions
3 sherry glasses sherry
700 g (1½ lb) cooking
  apples
700 g (1½ lb) celery
1¾ liters (3¾ pints)
  water
2 teaspoons cumin
salt and pepper
125 ml (¼ pint) sour
  cream
almond cookies

Mali Pie

Fry onions in cooking oil for 10 minutes until soft and brown. Stir in peanuts, tomatoes, Worcestershire sauce, herbs, and seasoning. Boil for 2–3 minutes to reduce tomato juice if necessary. Leave to cool. Meanwhile rub fat into flour to make pastry and bind with water. Roll out and line two 20 cm (8 in) pie plates. Place half the peanut mixture in each pie and cover with a pastry crust. Fork the edges and prick the center. Bake at 200°C/400°F for about 45 minutes or until the pastry is cooked.

Pastry
225 g (8 oz) plain flour
100 g (4 oz) butter
salt
water

Filling
350 g (12 oz) onions
350 g (12 oz) ground roast
  peanuts
1 large can tomatoes or 12
  fresh tomatoes
2 tablespoons marjoram
2 teaspoons
  Worchestershire sauce
cooking oil

Artichoke and Egg Flan

Make pastry by rubbing fat into flour and salt. Bind with a little water. Allow to rest and then roll out to line two 20 cm (8 in) flan cases. Bake for 8–10 minutes (do not open oven door during this period). Remove from oven and cover base with sliced artichoke hearts and cottage cheese. Season very well. Beat eggs with milk and pour over the top. Bake at 200°C/400°F for 1 hour until the flan is set and slightly browned.

Pastry
150 g (6 oz) plain flour
75 g (3 oz) butter
salt
water

Filling
12 artichoke hearts
225 g (8 oz) cottage
   cheese
4 eggs
250 ml (½ pint) milk
salt and pepper

Sprouts with Nutmeg

Remove outside leaves of sprouts and steam or simmer in salted water. Drain and dot with butter. Sprinkle with nutmeg and serve.

1½ kg (3 lb) sprouts
water
nutmeg
salt
butter

Potatoes Provençale

Melt butter with oil in a large frying pan. Fry finely chopped garlic and diced potatoes in the fat till soft. Serve sprinkled with chopped parsley.

1½ kg (3 lb) potatoes
2 cloves garlic
2 tablespoons parsley
25 g (1 oz) butter
45 ml (3 tablespoons)
   cooking oil

Apricots in Ginger

Wash apricots well and soak overnight in 250 ml (½ pint) of ginger wine, white wine, and enough water to cover. Pour into a large pan and bring to boil. Simmer for 20–30 minutes until apricots are cooked but not falling apart. Allow to cool and transfer to a glass dish. Top with remaining 125 ml (¼ pint) ginger wine and serve with fresh cream.

900g (2 lb) dried apricots
375ml (¾ pint) ginger
   wine
500ml (1 pint) white wine
water

Senegal Eggs
Lancashire Cheese Log with Pasta Salad, Grape
and Fennel Salad, and American Corn Bread
Avocado Chartreuse

Senegal Eggs

Halve hard-boiled eggs and arrange on a large plate.
Mix peanut butter with juice of 3 oranges and a little
orange rind. Add a little water if the mixture is too
thick. It should pour easily over the eggs. Garnish with
orange slices and watercress around the edge of the
plate.

12 hard-boiled eggs
4 tablespoons peanut
  butter
3 oranges
1 sliced orange for
  garnish
1 bunch watercress

Lancashire Cheese Log

Finely chop gherkins and olives and mix all ingredients
together. Bind with mayonnaise and a little cream to
make a stiffish mixture. Shape into 2 rolls and wrap in
greaseproof paper. Chill and serve sliced on a bed of
lettuce.

700 g (1½ lb) Lancashire
  cheese
6 small gherkins
8 stuffed olives
1 tablespoon chopped
  chives
1 teaspoon thyme
1 teaspoon French
  mustard
salt and black pepper
90 ml (6 tablespoons)
  mayonnaise
a little cream
lettuce

166

Pasta Salad

Cook pasta in boiling, salted water for about 20 minutes. Drain and allow to cool. Shred pepper and chop apple and celery. Mix all ingredients together and sprinkle with marjoram.

225 g (8 oz) mixed pasta shapes
100 g (4 oz) cooked soya beans
½ green pepper
1 apple
3 sticks celery
45 ml (3 tablespoons) oil and vinegar dressing
marjoram
salt and pepper

Grape and Fennel Salad

Parboil sliced fennel for 5 minutes. Drain and leave to cool. Halve and stone grapes and mix with chopped fennel. Add sour cream and salt and pepper and garnish with mint.

3 large fennel hearts
450 g (1 lb) green grapes
125 ml (¼ pint) sour cream
salt and pepper
2 sprigs of mint

American Corn Bread

Beat eggs and milk together and dissolve honey in the mixture. Add oil and pour over the dry ingredients. Stir well and pour into 2 well-greased 20 × 20 cm (8 × 8 in) square pans and bake in a moderate oven for about 1 hour.

275 g (10 oz) polenta or yellow cornmeal
150 g (6 oz) plain flour
90 ml (6 tablespoons) corn oil
4 tablespoons honey
2 eggs
400 ml (16 fl.oz) milk
2 teaspoons salt
4 teaspoons baking powder

Avocado Chartreuse

Whip 625 ml (1¼ pints) of heavy cream with sugar and
Chartreuse until stiff. Peel and stone avocados and
sieve quickly into cream mixture. Stir well and pour
into individual dishes. Decorate with angelica and a
little more whipped cream and serve as soon as possible as the avocado has a slight tendency to discolor.

6 avocados
750 ml (1½ pints) heavy
  cream
6 tablespoons sugar or
  honey
3 miniature bottles green
  Chartreuse
angelica

menu

Beanshoot Salad with Cream Cheese Dressing
Mexican Baked Spinach with Jollof Rice
and Aubergine Corn
Hazelnut Ice Cream with Poached Pears

Beanshoot Salad
with Cream Cheese Dressing

Dice cucumber, mushrooms, and green pepper and
mix with all other ingredients. Season. To make dressing mix cream cheese with milk until fairly runny. Add
chopped parsley to dressing. Season to taste. Chill and
pour over the salad. Serve at once.

350 g (12 oz) beanshoots
100 g (4 oz) mushrooms
  (smallish)
1 green pepper
½ cucumber
1 bunch watercress

Dressing
225 g (8 oz) cream cheese
90 ml (6 tablespoons)
  milk
4 tablespoons chopped
  parsley

Mexican Baked Spinach

Wash spinach and steam in a large pan for 5 minutes until the size is reduced considerably. Slice green peppers and blanch for 5 minutes in boiling water. Finely chop onions and celery and fry in cooking oil with cinnamon, Cayenne pepper, and dill seed for 5 minutes. Place half the spinach in the base of a large oval earthenware dish. Add a layer of peppers and then all the onion and celery mixture. Sprinkle with half the cheese and cover with remaining peppers. Next add remaining spinach and top with grated cheese. Sprinkle each layer with seasoning as you go. Bake at 190°C/375°F for 45 minutes.

2¾ kg (6 lbs) spinach
4 green peppers
2 large onions
½ head celery
100 g (4 oz) raisins
1 teaspoon cinnamon
½ teaspoon Cayenne
  pepper
½ teaspoon dill seed
125 ml (¼ pint) tomato
  juice
225 g (8 oz) grated cheese
salt and pepper
cooking oil

Jollof Rice

Finely chop onions and sauté in cooking oil till soft and beginning to brown. Add rice and continue to cook for 10 minutes, stirring from time to time. Stir in raisins, can of tomatoes, seasoning, and stock. Cook for about 30 minutes until rice is tender and the liquid just absorbed. Add peanuts and cook for a further 5 minutes, stirring from time to time.

350 g (12 oz) rice
450 g (1 lb) onions
100 g (4 oz) roast peanuts
50 g (2 oz) raisins or
  sultanas
450 g (1 lb) can tomatoes
250 ml (½ pint) vegetable
  stock
¼ teaspoon Cayenne
  pepper
¼ teaspoon salt
cooking oil

Aubergine Corn

Slice aubergines in rings and sauté in cooking oil. Layer in a casserole with corn and peeled tomatoes, seasoning each layer as you go. Sprinkle with bread crumbs and dot with butter. Bake at 190°C/375°F for 45 minutes.

6 medium aubergines
2 large cans Mexicorn
450 g (1 lb) tomatoes
100 g (4 oz) bread crumbs
butter
salt and pepper
cooking oil

Hazelnut Ice Cream

Whisk eggs with runny honey till thick and pale in color. Whip milk and cream until really stiff. Add ground hazelnuts quickly and fold in the egg mixture. Pour into container and freeze. To serve, spoon into individual dishes and sprinkle with grated chocolate.

9 eggs
3 tablespoons runny honey
375 ml (¾ pint) heavy cream
250 ml (½ pint) milk
150 g (6 oz) ground hazelnuts
1 small bar plain chocolate

Poached Pears

Peel, halve, and core pears and poach gently in white wine and honey for 20 minutes. Allow to cool and chill slightly before serving.

6 Conference pears
125 ml (¼ pint) white wine
1 tablespoon honey

menu

New England Jellied Vegetables
Savory Herb Quiche, Oat, Cheese, and Tomato
Flan with Cauliflower Salad, and Sweet Corn
and Watercress Salad
Gaelic Coffee Ice Cream Gâteau

New England Jellied Vegetables

Slice eggs and vegetables. Dissolve gelatine and mix with warm water and Marmite or sprinkle agar-agar over boiling water and Marmite. Allow to cool but not to set. Pour a little of the mixture into a gratin dish and place in refrigerator to set. Arrange the egg, olives, and gherkins on the jelly base and arrange the remaining vegetables and egg on top. Cover with the rest of the jelly and place in refrigerator to set. Alternatively arrange the eggs and vegetables in individual dishes and set the jelly in these. Turn out to serve and decorate with parsley.

275 g (10 oz) can cut asparagus
400 g (14 oz) can celery
2 hard-boiled eggs
4 cooked and peeled new potatoes
2 large gherkins
4 stuffed olives
2 teaspoons agar-agar or 12½ g (½ oz) gelatine
750 ml (¾ pint) water
1 teaspoon Marmite or yeast extract
parsley

Savory Herb Quiche

Make pastry by rubbing butter into flour and salt. Bind with water. Allow to rest and then roll out to line two 20 cm (8 in) flan pans. Grate cheese and mix with beaten eggs, cream, and milk. Add herbs and seasoning and pour half the mixture into each flan case. Bake at 200°C/400°F for about 1 hour until golden brown on top and cooked through the center. Allow to cool.

Pastry
150 g (6 oz) plain flour
75 g (3 oz) butter
salt
water

Filling
6 eggs
225 g (8 oz) Cheddar cheese
250 ml (½ pint) heavy cream
125 ml (¼ pint) milk
½ teaspoon each of thyme, tarragon, marjoram, basil
1 tablespoon freshly chopped parsley
salt and black pepper

Oat, Cheese, and Tomato Flan

Make pastry by rubbing butter into flour, salt, and oats. Bind with a little water. Press into two 20 cm (8 in) flan pans. Finely chop onions and fry in cooking oil until transparent. Mix with nuts, cheese, tomato paste, seasoning, and beaten eggs and fill each flan case. Bake at 200°C/400°F for about 45 minutes. Allow to cool.

Pastry
100 g (4 oz) butter
100 g (4 oz) rolled oats
100 g (4 oz) plain flour
water
salt

Filling
4 large onions
225 g (8 oz) grated Edam
  cheese
100 g (4 oz) ground
  hazelnuts
4 tablespoons tomato
  paste
60 ml (4 tablespoons)
  heavy cream
3 eggs
salt and pepper
cooking oil

Cauliflower Salad

Clean the cauliflowers and discard the stems. Divide into florets and immerse in oil and vinegar dressing. Leave for 2 hours. Finely chop other ingredients and mix with drained cauliflower, orange juice, and black pepper. Serve in a bowl lined with lettuce.

2 small young
  cauliflowers
125 ml (¼ pint) oil and
  vinegar dressing
1 head celery
2 red peppers
4 large gherkins
1 onion
juice of 2 oranges
black pepper
1 lettuce

Sweet Corn
and Watercress Salad

Coarsely chop washed and drained watercress and mix with drained sweet corn. Toss in dressing and sprinkle with black pepper.

3 bunches watercress
2 × 175 g (7 oz) cans Mexicorn
45 ml (3 tablespoons) oil and vinegar dressing
black pepper

Gaelic Coffee Ice Cream Gâteau

Whip cream, coffee, and sugar until as stiff as it will go. Dissolve honey in whisky and whisk with cream until as stiff as possible. Place half the coffee mixture in a square solid-based cake pan and place in freezer. When set, cover with half the gaelic ice cream mixture and return to freezer. Follow with another layer of each, freezing between each addition. If the cream mixtures start to separate before they are added to the layer cake, rewhip. Freeze cake. Just before serving, decorate with whipped cream and flaked almonds.

Coffee Ice Cream
250 ml (½ pint) heavy cream
100 g (4 oz) Barbados or molasses sugar
150 ml (5 fl.oz) coffee made with 1½ tablespoons instant coffee

Gaelic Ice Cream
250 ml (½ pint) heavy cream
1 tablespoon honey
60 ml (4 tablespoons) whisky

Decoration
125 ml (¼ pint) heavy cream
flaked almonds

Melon and Avocado Salad
Borlotti Vegetable Casserole
with Tarragon Rice and Red Cabbage Salad
Rhubarb and Walnut Ginger Crumble

Melon
and Avocado Salad

Mix dressing ingredients. Peel and cube melon and avocados and mix with dressing immediately to prevent discoloration of the avocados. Chill for 30 minutes and serve in individual bowls with a little watercress.

1 honeydew melon
4 large avocados
1 bunch watercress

Dressing
juice of 3 lemons
125 ml (¼ pint) corn oil
1 tablespoon freshly
    chopped mint
black pepper

Tarragon Rice

Cook rice in boiling salted water until tender. Drain well and mix with tarragon. Serve dotted with knobs of butter.

800 g (1 lb 12 oz) rice
1 tablespoon tarragon
salt
water
butter

Borlotti
Vegetable Casserole

Soak Borlotti beans overnight. Finely slice onion and fry in cooking oil in a large pan until it starts to turn transparent. Add flour and continue cooking for 2–3 minutes, stirring all the time. Gradually add vegetable stock, still stirring, and bring to boil. Add beans, herbs, seasoning, and Marmite. Simmer for 45 minutes. Peel and slice carrots, wash and slice celery, and wash and separate cauliflower florets. Add to the beans with parsley, white wine, and sufficient water to just about cover the vegetables with the sauce. Bring back to boil and simmer for another ½–¾ hour until all the beans and vegetables are cooked through. Correct seasoning and serve.

350 g (12 oz) dried
  Borlotti beans
6 onions
6 tablespoons plain flour
1½ liters (3 pints)
  vegetable stock
2 teaspoons Marmite or
  yeast extract
cooking oil
2 teaspoons celery seed
  or salt
1 teaspoon tarragon
2 teaspoons marjoram
black pepper
350 g (12 oz) shelled
  broad beans
6 carrots
1 head celery
1 cauliflower
300 ml (12 fl.oz) white
  wine
300 ml (12 fl.oz) water
3 tablespoons chopped
  parsley

Red Cabbage Salad

Finely shred red cabbage and mix with very finely chopped celery and onion. Toss in dressing and season to taste.

1 red cabbage
4 sticks celery
1 small onion
90 ml (6 tablespoons) oil
  and vinegar dressing
salt and pepper

Rhubarb and Walnut Ginger Crumble

Wash and chop rhubarb and place in a pan with sugar or honey, lemon juice, and sufficient water to cover about two-thirds of the rhubarb. Bring to boil and simmer for 10 minutes or until the rhubarb is soft. Make the crumble topping by rubbing the fat into the flour and mixing with nuts, sugar, and ginger. Place rhubarb in a large oval dish and sprinkle on the crumble, pressing down lightly. Bake at 180°C/350°F for about 40–45 minutes until golden brown.

1½ kg (3 lb) rhubarb
6 tablespoons Barbados sugar or honey
juice of 1 lemon
100 g (4 oz) raisins

Topping
400 g (14 oz) plain flour
225 g (8 oz) butter or margarine
225 g (8 oz) sugar
100 g (4 oz) chopped walnuts
½ teaspoon ground ginger

Catering for a Cocktail Party 12

This chapter includes canapés, dips, and hot savories. The recipes are all for 24 people, given a selection of 5 or 6 items for the party.

The canapés are served cold, arranged on decorative plates, or on paper doilies either mixed or separately.

The dips should be served in bowls surrounded by smaller bowls of cruditée, small cheese crackers, and toast rounds. Cruditée would include long, slim wedges of carrot, cucumber, celery, and spring onions, as well as cauliflower florets and olives.

The savories are all served hot with toothpicks to handle them.

Canapés

Pinwheels*

Mix cream cheese with sufficient cream to give a smooth, thick, creamy consistency. Divide into 2 batches and mix one with sesame seeds and the other with rosemary. Season each batch to taste. Spread thinly sliced bread that has had its crusts removed with the cream cheese mixtures. Roll up lengthways and slice into 6 pinwheels per slice.

8 large slices bread
350 g (12 oz) cream cheese
60 ml (4 tablespoons) cream
2 teaspoons toasted ground sesame seeds
2 teaspoons rosemary
salt and pepper

Cucumber Crowns**

Slice cucumber into 48 rounds. Hard boil and slice eggs. Halve stuffed olives. Arrange cucumber on a large plate and place a slice of egg on each piece. Top with half a stuffed olive and sprinkle with paprika pepper.

1 large cucumber
6 eggs
24 stuffed olives
paprika pepper

Almond and Onion Pâté Savories

Chop onions as finely as possible and gently fry in a little of the butter until soft and lightly browned. Mix with remaining butter until smooth and runny. Add almonds, herbs, and seasoning and spoon into a dish. Leave to set. Spread on slices of toast and cut each slice into 8 pieces.

6 large slices toast
3 onions
75 g (3 oz) butter
125 g (5 oz) ground almonds
1 teaspoon celery seed
1 teaspoon summer savory
salt and pepper

*See Plate 8 (2nd and 7th rows).

**See Plate 8 (5th row).

178

Stuffed Dates*

Mix cream cheese with mayonnaise and add sesame and seasoning. Stone dates and fill with cream cheese mixture. Push a stuffed olive or a quarter walnut into the center of each date.

48 dates
125 g (5 oz) cream cheese
1 teaspoon toasted ground sesame seeds
10–15 ml (2–3 teaspoons) mayonnaise
salt and pepper
24 stuffed olives
24 walnut quarters

Mali Canapés**

Mix all ingredients together with mayonnaise to bind. Chill for an hour and then spread onto slices of toast. Cut each piece into 6 squares and serve sprinkled with chopped parsley.

8 slices toast
100 g (4 oz) grated Cheddar cheese
50 g (2 oz) roasted peanuts
25 g (1 oz) chopped raisins
30 ml (2 tablespoons) mayonnaise
salt and pepper

Orange Cheese Truffles***

Finely chop dates, raisins, and almonds and mix with cream cheese. Add grated rind of one orange and mixed spice with enough orange juice to make a stiff paste. Mix well and chill for 4–6 hours. Remove from refrigerator and shape into about 100 small balls. Roll in toasted ground sesame seeds. Slice remaining oranges in slim wedges and arrange on a large plate with the cheese truffles.

450 g (1 lb) soft cream cheese
225 g (8 oz) dates
225 g (8 oz) raisins
150 g (6 oz) flaked almonds
30 ml (2 tablespoons) orange juice
1 teaspoon mixed spice
3–4 tablespoons toasted ground sesame seeds
7 oranges

*See Plate 8 (3rd and 8th rows).
**See Plate 8 (4th and 9th rows).
***See Plate 8 (1st and 6th rows).

Dips

Indian Curry Dip

Soak chick peas in water overnight and drain well. Fry
onion, garlic, and spices in butter until onions start to
soften. Add chick peas and flour and stir well. Add
water and bring to boil. Simmer for 1½–2 hours until
the peas are soft. Allow to cool and pass through a
mouli. Mix with cream cheese and milk to form a
smooth creamy paste. Add more curry powder to taste.

150 g (6 oz) chick peas
1 onion
1 tablespoon flour
2 cloves garlic
1 piece stem ginger
2 green chilis without
  seeds
1 teaspoon turmeric
½ teaspoon coriander
25 g (1 oz) butter
375 ml (¾ pint) water
salt and pepper
350 g (12 oz) cream
  cheese
150 ml (6 fl.oz) milk
½ teaspoon curry
  powder, optional

Garlic Dip

Crush garlic in a little salt and add to mayonnaise. Add
lemon juice and plenty of black pepper to taste.

225 g (8 oz) mayonnaise
4 cloves garlic
juice of 1 lemon
black pepper
salt

Mexican Dip

Fry coarsely chopped onion and green pepper in cooking oil until fairly soft. Drain beans and pass through a mouli with the onion and pepper. Add all other ingredients and mix to a smooth creamy paste.

450 g (1 lb) can lima
  beans
½ green pepper
1 small onion
1 tablespoon tomato
  paste
75 ml (3 fl.oz) cream
150 ml (6 fl.oz) tomato
  juice
juice of half a lemon
10–15 ml (2–3 teaspoons)
  Worcestershire sauce
paprika
garlic salt
black pepper
cooking oil

Sesame and Chutney Dip

Blend all ingredients with a fork, adding a little more milk if necessary to give a creamy consistency.

450 g (1 lb) cream cheese
3 tablespoons blended
  chutney
1 tablespoon toasted
  ground sesame seeds
salt and pepper
a little milk

Peanut Dip

Blend all ingredients with a fork, adding milk gradually to achieve a smooth creamy consistency.

450 g (1 lb) cream cheese
150 ml (6 fl.oz) milk
4 tablespoons peanut
  butter
30 ml (2 tablespoons)
  cream

Chick Pea
and Sesame Dip

Cook chick peas (see Chapter 4). Rub through a sieve and mix with ground sesame seeds. Add lemon juice and crushed cloves of garlic. Stir in the salad oil just before serving and sprinkle with chopped parsley. Serve with small pieces of hot Greek bread.

700 g (1½ lb) chick peas
375 g (13 oz) sesame
  seeds
250 ml (½ pint) salad oil
12 lemons
4 cloves garlic
4 tablespoons finely
  chopped parsley
Greek bread

Egg and Avocado Dip

Peel and mash avocados. Add lemon juice and mayonnaise. Peel, deseed, and chop tomatoes and finely chop or sieve eggs and add to the mixture. Season to taste and serve on a bed of lettuce, sprinkled with paprika pepper.

5 avocados
12 hard-boiled eggs
6 tomatoes
90 ml (6 tablespoons)
  lemon juice
90 ml (6 tablespoons)
  mayonnaise
paprika pepper
salt and pepper
3–4 lettuce leaves

Artichoke Dip

Sieve the artichoke hearts and mix with lemon juice. Stir in mayonnaise and season to taste.

12 artichoke hearts
225 g (8 oz) mayonnaise
juice of 1 lemon
salt and pepper

Savories

Spiced Lentil Tartlets

Fry finely chopped onion with garlic and spices for 5 minutes. Wash lentils and add to onions. Cover with water and add all other filling ingredients. Bring to boil and simmer until the lentils are cooked and the mixture is fairly thick, about 1–1½ hours. Meanwhile rub fat into flour and salt and bind with water. Roll out fairly thinly and line 24 small tart pans with pastry. Place a spoonful of cold filling in each tart and cover with a pastry lid. Bake at 200°C/400°F for about 35–40 minutes until the pastry is beginning to brown. Serve hot.

Pastry
225 g (8 oz) plain flour
100 g (4 oz) butter
salt
water

Filling
100 g (4 oz) lentils
500 ml (1 pint) water
1 teaspoon Marmite or
   yeast extract
1 large onion
1 clove garlic
1 tablespoon tomato
   paste
½ teaspoon chili powder
¼ teaspoon ground
   cumin seed
½ teaspoon thyme
¼ teaspoon allspice
salt and pepper
cooking oil

Camembert Gems

Make a thick roux with the flour, butter, and milk and add grated Camembert, tarragon, and seasoning. Allow to cool with greaseproof paper over the top. Spoon out small balls and roll in egg and then in bread crumbs and deep fry. Do not leave in the fat too long or the cheese will cause the balls to run. For a milder taste, use Brie cheese.

450 g (1 lb) Camembert
100 g (4 oz) flour
100 g (4 oz) butter
625 ml (1¼) pints milk
2 teaspoons tarragon
salt and pepper
3 eggs
100–150 g (4–6 oz) fine
   bread crumbs

183

Bibliography

Manual of Nutrition, Ministry of Agriculture, Fisheries and Food, HMSO, 1976.

The Facts of Food, Arnold E. Bender, Oxford University Press, 1975.

Let's Eat Right To Keep Fit, Adelle Davis, Unwin Paperbacks, 1974.

The Loaf and the Law, Kenneth Barlow, Precision Press.

Eating Your Way to Health, Ruth Bircher, Faber and Faber Ltd., 1966.

Diet For a Small Planet, Frances Moore Lappe, Ballantine Books (New York), 1976.

Nutrition: Better Health through Good Eating, Sheila Bingham, Corgi Paperbacks.

"Repair function of cholesterol versus the lipid theory of arteriosclerosis," Hans Kaunitz, *Chemistry and Industry*, September 17, 1977.

"Diet-Heart: End of an Era," George V. Mann, *New England Journal of Medicine*, September 22, 1977.

"Your Diet and your Heart," Sir John McMichael, *Home Economics*, November 1977.

"Arteriosclerosis—a cause for concern," Dr. Malcolm Parry, *Home Economics*, April 1978.

184

Index